THE DEMONS HAVE HAD IT

THE DEMONS HAVE HAD IT

A Theological ABC

By Charles Scriven

Southern Publishing Association, Nashville, Tennessee

 Library of Congress Catalog Card No. 76-2926. SBN 8127-0111-9.

This book was edited by Richard Coffen, designed by Dean Tucker. The cover was illustrated by Lane Yerkes. Text set 10/12 Palatino. Printed in U.S.A.

All Scriptural references in this book are quoted from the Revised Standard Version.

Dedication

To my parents, who passed on the Good News to my brothers and me.

Table of Contents

Before the Book Begins

There is no need to talk about the title. Its meaning will become clear as you read what is inside. But the subtitle calls the book a theological ABC, and I do want to talk about that.

In the first place, the subtitle means that the book deals with theology. It discusses what concerns us all the most: our eternal meaning and destiny as persons. It talks about where we've come from, who we are, and where we're going. And because of this, it is not primarily a book of stories and illustrations but a book of ideas. On these pages you will read about the main themes of Christian understanding.

In the second place, the subtitle means that this book tries to explain its subject matter in easy-to-read terms. It has as little technical jargon as possible, because I have written a book, not for professional theologians (who are still welcome to read it) but for ordinary, thoughtful persons who want to learn more about the Christian faith.

There is another thing. The subtitle is my way of

disavowing any pretense of academic scholarship. My role here is that of middleman, someone who tries to make theological scholarship (or what I know of it) available in a concise and digestible form. This, too, is risky business, but I have done it anyway, partly because it is fun and partly to try, in my own way, to be useful in God's creation.

The book has been my principal hobby for some time, and I want to thank my wife, Marianne, for helping and loving me during this period. I am also grateful to Jonathan, our three-year-old. In trying to urge me away from the typewriter so that we could play, he was often rebuffed, but never did he let his disappointment fester into a grudge.

I also want to thank Roberta J. Moore for teaching me to respect and love the English sentence and Roy Branson, Edward Vick, and Herold Weiss for teaching me the joys of theological reflection. They will all feel relieved, however, if I tell you that their principal influence upon me occurred long enough ago that they cannot be blamed for my mistakes.

CHARLES SCRIVEN

Chapter 1

A Life Worth Living:
The Book Begins

How can we find meaning for our lives?

This question, more than any other, has engaged and tantalized the human imagination in our century. Ours is an age of agony and hope, and this is a question of agony and hope. It points alike to the discontent and flaming dreams of the human spirit. No one can ask it without being catapulted from the countryside of easy nonchalance to that inner city where the deepest riddles of existence are as impossible to ignore as the shadows on the streets. Is there some worth to our lives, some hope? Or are we specks of insignificance, and is our striving folly?

If one thing terrifies us more than death, it is life itself when life is not worth living. Viktor Frankl, a Vienna psychiatrist who survived the Nazi concentration camps, knew this well, as he shows in a beautiful and painful story from his days as a prisoner: "F——, my senior block warden, a fairly well-known composer and librettist, confided in me one day: 'I would like to tell you something, Doctor. I have had a strange dream. A voice told me that I could wish for something, that I should only say what I wanted to know, and all my questions would be answered. What do you think I asked? That I would like to know when the war would be over for me. You know what I mean, Doctor—for me! I wanted to know when we, when our camp, would be liberated and our sufferings come to an end.'

" 'And when did you have this dream?' I asked.

" 'In February, 1945,' he answered. It was then the beginning of March.

" 'What did your dream voice answer?'

"Furtively he whispered to me, 'March thirtieth.'

"When F—— told me about his dream, he was still full of hope and convinced that the voice of his dream would be right. But as the promised day drew nearer, the war news which reached our camp made it appear very unlikely that we would be free on the promised date. On March twenty-ninth, F—— suddenly became ill and ran a high temperature. On March thirtieth, the day his prophecy had told him that the war and suffering would be over for him, he became delirious and lost consciousness. On March thirty-first, he was dead. To all outward appearances, he had died of typhus."[1]

Frankl insists that the ultimate cause of his friend's death was the severe disappointment, which lowered his body's resistance against the disease. The story underscores the truth that nothing is so unbearable as seeing our dreams reduced to nightmares. When hope leaves, so does life, or at least the vitality of life. The freedom we want more than any other is freedom from loss of meaning.

A Life Worth Living: The Book Begins

Down through time there has been a whole syllabus of different approaches to finding a meaningful life. All offer one form or another of comfort and peace, and all hinge on a certain way of experiencing Ultimate Reality, or what we call God. One of these approaches is Christianity,* the subject of this book.

Many people imagine that Christianity is old, familiar stuff. We belong to a Judeo-Christian culture, which seems to imply that we know enough already of Christianity. But, in fact, there is much ignorance of Christian belief. Outside the churches, for example, you can find this ignorance and misunderstanding just about anywhere you wish to look.

If you can find a cocksure bricklayer who, by pronouncing Christianity unscientific, considers himself to have toppled organized religion, you can also find a Yale professor who mocks Christianity as "just another form of giving up the present for some goal."[2]

If you can find a beginning philosophy student who thinks Christianity is demolished by the claim that it is based on wishful thinking, you can also find a Chicago playboy who insists that Christian morals suck all the fun out of life.

By a kind of oversight, even many people within the churches have not acquired anything like a well-rounded understanding of their religion. That is one reason why you can find churchgoing, teetotaling, racist warmongers in America and rich Christian liberals, with

*The understanding of Christianity presented in this book of course reflects my own perspective, which is Protestant and Seventh-day Adventist.

a fine sense of justice, who spend their wealth mainly on themselves while the poor continue to suffer.

With this problem in mind, I have written a very short book about Christianity. It is not a complete account, only a beginning of sorts—a cup of water, not the reservoir. I intend simply that my readers taste what (as far as I can tell) Christian faith really is, instead of what popular caricatures make it out to be. I want to show what it means for our existence now—to say, among other things, that it is indeed not "just another form of giving up the present for some goal."

I will talk a great deal about God. In particular, I will talk much of Jesus Christ, for He, Christians believe, reveals God. Through Him Christians experience Ultimate Reality and find meaning for their lives.

At this point I will say little about Him—except that there was something altogether striking about the way He lived and talked. Those who followed Him came under the conviction that He was a messiah, someone who would save His people. Although His crucifixion blasted apart their hopes, a few days later they were convinced that Jesus had survived the tomb. And their hopes, indeed their lives, revived.

Sixty years later when John wrote his Gospel, he reported that Jesus had told them, " 'I am the way, and the truth, and the life' " (John 14:6). He had said, referring to Himself, " 'If the Son makes you free, you will be free indeed' " (John 8:36). Jesus had not merely theorized about truth, life, and freedom, He offered these things —offered, in short, a life worth living. Sixty years after Jesus' death, people remembered that He had addressed

Himself to the ultimate concerns of the human race. Sixty years after His death, they believed in their deepest selves that God above had somehow been at work through Him and was still working through Him.

Later we will talk about why this happened, why people began taking this astonishing attitude toward an ex-carpenter from Nazareth. We will look in more detail at what it means, but first I want to consider another important question. In the modern world, one may choose from numerous approaches to the finding of meaning—as different from one another as, say, idol worship and atheism. How does the Christian's approach compare with these? What is it—really!—that sets Christianity apart?

Of course, no answer short of a very long book would be adequate here. But it is possible to indicate a useful vantage point from which to reflect on how the Christian experience of Ultimate Reality differs from the others. This is what I want to do before the main part of the book begins.

As theologian John Macquarrie suggests, two somewhat technical terms provide us with such a vantage point.[3] One is *transcendence,* which refers to the idea that God, or Ultimate Reality, is beyond or separate from the material universe. A transcendent God is one who is radically different from the tangible world, from what you see, hear, touch, feel, and smell. He is above the world. He is independent of it.

Some religions see God as so transcendent, so far away from the tangible world, that He becomes remote and disinterested. The Chinese religion of

Confucianism is an example. God receives polite recognition, but has little to do with human affairs. The philosopher Hsün-Tzu went so far as to say that Heaven conducts itself without any relation to the world.

Jewish monotheism also sees God as transcendent. As our maker He is superior to the material universe and is ruler over it. Yet God at the same time involves Himself with the world. He draws near to it, as He did in the Exodus, for example, in order to save it.

This quality in the Jewish conception of God takes us to the second word, *immanence,* which refers to the idea that God is within the world and its processes. Some religions stress the immanence of God so strongly that little transcendence remains. In pantheism, the view of certain Eastern religions, God is in all things and all things are part of God; there is no personal, sovereign Reality outside the material universe.

The point I want to make is that Christianity, like its closest neighbor, Judaism, combines these emphases. "In the beginning was the Word, and the Word was with God, and the Word was God. . . . All things were made through him," writes John, expressing the Christian vision of God as our transcendent Maker. Then he adds—here is the radical immanence in the Christian view—"And the Word became flesh and dwelt among us" (John 1:1-3, 14).

You will see as you read this book that the Christian answer to the problem of meaning turns on this astonishing vision of God. God is transcendent—independent of the material universe and, therefore, ruler over it. From a position of power He can fulfill His purposes. At the same time, God is immanent—neither distant nor aloof, but present in the world and in our very lives. Out of choice—out of love!—God is within His creation; we can experience communion with the Divine.

You can keep this perspective in mind as you read this book (or, perhaps, look seriously at non-Christian views of life). The experience of God as One *beyond* but who from love is at work *within* has fueled the church through the ages. It solves the problem of meaning for Christians and sets Christianity apart. The implications of this experience will unfold, if only sketchily, through the rest of this brief volume.

---

[1] Viktor E. Frankl, *Man's Search for Meaning* (Boston: Beacon Press, 1962), pp. 74, 75.

[2] Charles Reich, *The Greening of America* (New York: Random House, 1970), p. 301.

[3] See John Macquarrie, *Principles of Christian Theology* (New York: Charles Scribner's Sons, 1966), pp. 146-155.

Chapter 2

The Living God: *Affirming Faith in the Modern Age*

As you have seen, it is impossible to say anything at all about Christianity without referring to God. I have just written about the great itch for meaning that all human beings share and have said something of how the Christian approach to finding a meaningful life differs from other approaches. In so doing, I produced a chapter filled with the mention of God. Indeed, no matter what subject I might consider, whether sex, politics, the rodeo, or rock music, if I am a Christian with God as the absolute center of all meaning and value for me, my views must ultimately include some kind of reference to Him.

We must ask now just what all this talk about God means. The modern spectator, looking on from outside the Christian faith, often puzzles skeptically over the Christian's belief. The reality of God is not scientifically demonstrable. The old "logical proofs of His existence" have a certain value as testimony, but they will hardly do as proofs. The modern man or woman knows very well, for example, that if the grandeur of a landscape or the beauty of a newborn child suggests to some the existence of a loving designer, others notice landscapes torn by disaster and babies born without arms or without sight and wonder what these are supposed to suggest about God.

Yet even though God seems hidden and evil lacerates our world, the Christian continues to confess his belief. Even the charge that "God is just a crutch for the insecure" does not extinguish the Christian's faith, nor does the common saying that we today, being advanced in knowledge, have outgrown the religion of our ancestors. The Christian, despite all this, goes on believing.

The questions to which we now address ourselves are: (1) What does the Christian mean when he says, "I believe in God"? and (2) Why does he make this statement in the first place? I do not anticipate, of course, that I will cause everything to fall into place and make coming to faith an easy, commonsense thing to do. My job, instead, will be to confront the reader, as nearly as I am able, with what the Christian belief is and with why it can be reasonably affirmed in the modern age. The Bible offers the classic expression of what Christians believe, and we must go to that source at the beginning if we are to understand our topic.

Now, in the Bible, talk about God does not proceed simply from the theoretical assumption that there must be a divine world. The Bible writers were more like newspapermen than like speculative poets or philosophers. *They reported events—things they had seen and heard—and then explained the meaning of these events.* Of course, they were insiders. They did not watch and interpret from the sidelines in the manner of the modern-day objective reporter. But this difference must not obscure the main point: the Bible is primarily a record and interpretation of events, not a book of philosophical theories.

When the Bible writers wrote about God, they did not do so as part of a quest for some theoretical explanation of the universe. Instead, they wrote about God because He, on His own initiative, had acted in their community and in the events of their history. God had done something for them, and they had felt His presence. That is why, when God speaks in the Bible, He speaks as the God who acts. " 'I am the Lord your God, who brought you out of the land of Egypt, out of the house of bondage,' " He affirms in Exodus 20:2.

The Bible writers knew this God and worshiped Him as Lord only because He had entered into a saving relationship with them and their community. Moses and his people had been delivered from Egyptian bondage. The New Testament writers had been touched by the "event" of Jesus Christ. And all of them knew very well that there was "Someone there," that God Himself had taken the initiative on their behalf. They had experienced personally what Karl Barth has said, that this "is not a world left to itself but a world which He has loved and saved."[1]

For the Bible writers, then, the word *God* signified much more than some inner human essence—or potential—or the process of nature. God was a self—Someone who loved, who had a will, who took action. He was outside nature. He was independent of flesh and earth and sky. Yet He was personal—Someone you could love and trust.

Now the modern Christian, following his spiritual ancestors, believes in the same God, a God with the same personal interest and involvement in human affairs. As one of these Christians I must say, however, that I do not have a complete explanation of how I have come to know this God, any more than the agnostic has a complete explanation of his skepticism. I may clarify my views and give reasons for what I believe, as I intend to do in this chapter, but I cannot *prove* that I am right.

As the Bible writers simply declared their faith, that, in the last analysis, is what I must do. I belong to a community that has experienced God at work in the world, and what I say testifies to this. God has done something (this will occupy us more fully in later chapters), and it has affected me and my fellow believers. It has given us a new understanding of our moral obligations and of the purpose of our existence, as well as a new sense of optimism as we face the future.

As a Christian, I must say also that I do not claim to know anything about what God looks like, what He is made of, or how it happens that He is God. I do not have any inside information to enable me to describe "God as he is in himself."[2] I cannot, in other words, tell you about God in the abstract. I cannot say anything about Him apart from what He, through His Word and His deeds, has said about Himself. I can only describe God as He has revealed Himself to me and to the great community of people who have believed in Him down through the ages.

I share with my fellow believers—both of the past and of the present—a certain basic understanding of the God I worship. He is an "I," Someone who relates Himself to me and my fellow human beings something like the way one person relates to another. Yet He is not an ordinary "I" like Plato or Napoleon. For He is the very Maker of heaven and earth, the creative power in and beneath and beyond everything that is. Therefore He is infinitely superior to me, as well as to the universe where He has put me. I am indebted to Him for everything.

Even so—and here is a great wonder!—He loves me. He loves all people. He loves the whole creation. I am of such worth in His eyes, in fact, that He wants me to love Him back. He wants me and my fellow human beings to live in personal communion with Him. " 'And you shall love the Lord your God,' " He says, " 'with all your heart, and with all your soul, and with all your might' " (Deuteronomy 6:5). So if I do not know anything about "God as he is in himself," I do know this about His will: He has an unfailing disposition to be involved in human struggles and to bend all history—including my personal history—toward the triumph of life and love over death and hate.

This, roughly, is what the modern Christian has in mind when he says that he believes in God. Yet, precisely when he has finished expressing himself, the thinking individual will demand to know more about what the Christian really means. For in connection with the words of the Christian, a problem arises, and failure at this point to do some explaining might well imperil any attempt to communicate Christianity's doctrine of God.

Put briefly, the problem is that the modern Christian has no access to a language other than the human, yet he persists in talking about the divine. He uses words from the world of human ideas and human behavior to describe *God!* What he says about God, therefore, is humanlike. It assigns human qualities to Him who isn't human. And unless the Christian carefully explains what he means, all kinds of confusion and considerable nonsense result.

You can readily see that this is the case. When I say, for example, that God is personal, do I mean that He is a Big Man in the sky? No. That would be a quaint and obviously inadequate way of thinking about God. Instead, I mean that God is *at least* personal. Certainly there is much about Him that we cannot comprehend or even visualize. Yet whatever He may be beyond our human ability to comprehend, He is, at the very least, One who meets us and relates to us in a personal way.

I must make a similar clarification if I say, for example, that God is Lord. Do I mean that He is oppressive and overbearing, with a kind of imperial contempt for ordinary people? I do not. The word *Lord* expresses the conviction that God is absolutely in charge of things, that He rules the entire creation. It is not meant to contradict the belief that God is a God of love who has given personal freedom to all men and women and who has elected, despite human evil, to restore beauty and goodness and joy to the world.

The most serious question, perhaps, arises from the practice of referring to God in the masculine gender. The name *Father* and the pronoun *He* are examples of this. Does such masculine language mean that God is male? that maleness is somehow closer to divinity than femaleness? Feminists would say, Yes, those are the things men have always believed. And I think that, to a great degree, they are right. In any case, today it is necessary to say clearly that Christians do not mean (any longer, at least) to put forth an ideology of male superiority. In this book I still use words like *Father* and *He,* but only to emphasize (with Scripture) that God is personal instead of neuter. It is hard to be content with this. Someday changes in the English language will perhaps give us better ways to speak of God.

You might suppose that matters could be considerably improved if Christians would just get as far away as possible from humanlike language. Why not introduce abstract, philosophical terms for God and be done with the problem?

In truth, philosophical language does help, and Christian theologians have spoken of God, for example, as The Absolute, or as Being Itself. Yet these terms themselves derive from the realm of human experience, and there is no reason to think they are better than the more ordinary, personal terms in the Christian's vocabulary. If *Lord* and *Father* need explanation, so do the abstractions, which obscure what has always been the central conviction of the Christian faith; namely, that God is personal and that He involves Himself in human affairs. They suggest a cold, impersonal force in the universe rather than a God whose "steadfast love endures for ever" (Psalm 100:5).

The great mass of Christians believe that God has

approached the problems of this world in a personal and concrete way. He loves the world, making it possible for human beings to enjoy a personal relationship with Him, and He has given through the actual life of Jesus of Nazareth a concrete picture of His will. This is why personal, concrete language forms the people's language of the Christian faith. It means the most to the ordinary man and woman. If God Himself has chosen to relate to the world in the manner of a loving Father and a merciful and compassionate Friend, then the Christian may speak of Him as Father and as Friend. At the same time, he knows that he cannot literally identify God with any of the limited forms of existence that the human mind can comprehend.

The commandment says, " 'You shall not make for yourself a graven image, or any likeness of anything that is in heaven above, or that is in the earth beneath, or that is in the water under the earth; you shall not bow down to them or serve them' " (Exodus 20:4, 5). God is always more than any human language—whether words or sculpture or painting—can ever express. God is God—not one *thing* among other things. God is only Himself, and human language can never perfectly represent Him. Yet He has involved Himself in our affairs in such a way that what we really need to know about Him can be understood. If we cannot comprehend "God as he is in himself," we can comprehend His will. We can know enough about Him to respond one way or the other to His invitation that we love and trust Him.

When I began the present chapter, I said that neither

scientists nor logicians can verify God's existence. I must deal now with the obvious implication of this; namely, that no Christian can prove that God is not a mere figment of the imagination. The Christian cannot produce God to the skeptical world in the way that an archaeologist, for example, can produce the artifacts he claims to have found. As you may suppose, skeptics have been quick to seize upon this fact and to use it in their criticisms of the Christian faith. Among the best known of these criticisms—with Sigmund Freud its most celebrated advocate—is the view that God is just a mythological personality dreamed up to satisfy various psychological needs. Humanity needed someone to lean on, the argument goes, so it invented God.

What can the Christian say to this? One thing is certain: There is no way to refute categorically such an interpretation. But if called upon to prove its views, the opposition finds itself in a similar impasse. If the Christian cannot produce God for the benefit of skeptical onlookers, neither can the skeptics produce any proof that He is imaginary. So the critics certainly do not leave the Christian speechless. Indeed, there is considerable that he can say.

First of all, the Christian can point out that when he speaks of God, he is not merely giving voice to some private or eccentric opinion. As Richard Niebuhr said, the things the Christian feels certain about grow "out of immediate perception plus social corroboration and out of neither one of these alone."[3]

So while the Christian has, indeed, experienced God personally, a large community of other human beings down through millennia of history have had the same experience and have said, or are now saying, the same things. If the Christian cannot produce God, he can at least point to his fellow believers, all of whom would ardently testify that God is more than an invention. While the critics may dispute the testimony of a large community of people such as this, they certainly cannot ignore or dismiss it lightly.

In the second place, contrary to what the skeptics may say, the God of Christian faith is not cosmic cotton candy whipped up to take the edge off the troubles and misery of human existence. It is true that the faith of the Christian enables him to bear suffering and to live with hope, but that is not the whole story. God also makes uncomfortable demands. He asks the Christian for rigorous commitment to the needs of human beings and to the care of the earth. Nothing—not money, not romance, not career, not even family—may be allowed to interfere with this commitment. It is one thing to say, as Freud did, that God is an illusion. But to say that God is a *convenient* illusion, to say that He is a nice, genial, undemanding escape—*that* is nonsense.

More than this, the Christian may appeal to reason. Though he cannot make a neat, unimpeachable argument for Christianity, he can do what persons of other convictions can do: *describe* his faith, especially the central points, and explain what it means for human existence. Then he can ask whether the Christian view of life does not seem, despite all the difficulties, to make sense. (You will have to read the whole book, not just this chapter, to see how often Christian views agree with the common experience of men and women.)

A fourth response for the Christian is that of a life

lived in accord with what he believes. Suppose a cynic accuses you of using the person you love to satisfy your own need to be loved. Suppose he calls your love a charade. If he does this, you will never refute him by argument. He can label everything you say a "rationalization." But by the concrete ways in which you care for the person you love, by the everyday indications that you are not putting on, you make a powerful statement that your love is genuine. In the same way, the Christian whose life reflects what he believes makes a powerful statement that the Divine Reality he speaks of, far from being an illusion, is actually at work in his life.

Yet when the Christian has said all he can, he still falls short of proof for his views. But as I pointed out before, Freudians fall short of proof for their views—as do Marxists, Buddhists, and nudists. Our "deepest convictions . . . are rooted," as Gordon Kaufman has stated, "in a kind of unquestioned faith, not in logical demonstration."[4] In the end, the Christian must simply ask his listener to size up what has been said, to try to enter into it "sympathetically," and then to decide whether it is a true picture of our existence![5] The listener's decision is, in the end, a mystery—for the Marxist trying to win converts as surely as for the Christian.

Let's consider one more troublesome question before the chapter ends. If God really discloses Himself to the human race, how does it happen that only certain people are in the know and others are not? Why does a God of love and justice appear to play favorites?

The answer has to do with the kind of persons God

wants us to be. He made us (as the Creation story shows) with the ability to do unpredictable things out of our own personal initiative. He made us to be creatively involved in shaping the human story. We are free, decision-making beings, and in order to preserve our freedom, God has chosen not to overwhelm us with His presence. He does not want to present Himself so unmistakably that we have no choice but to acknowledge His authority over us. This would make our response to Him—and to life itself—as cold and automatic as our obedience to traffic lights. It would destroy our freedom. It would completely take away our initiative in the fulfillment of His purposes for the creation.

I have pointed out already that God's self-revelation has occurred in the form of liberating acts. Yet even when He delivered His people from Egyptian bondage and even when He acted in the life of Jesus, He remained the God who could be known, not by scientific observation or logical deduction but only by a religious experience of love and trust.

And so it should be no surprise that not everyone perceives what God is doing. God still works wherever there is faith and love and wherever there are victories over misery and pain. But His activity can be missed, even as many in the first century missed it during Jesus' ministry. No one is forced to commit himself to the Maker of all things. As Pascal wrote, "There is enough light for those who only desire to see, and enough obscurity for those who have a contrary disposition."[6]

We have dealt now with several questions concerning the Christian's faith in God, yet nothing I have said removes the mystery that surrounds the subject. The skeptic will still have questions to ask, and, indeed, the Christian himself knows these questions. He knows them well. The mystery of God, in the days of the modern believer as certainly as in the days of Job, " 'is longer than the earth, and broader than the sea' " (Job 11:9).

But the Christian has felt, along with others who believe, the impact of the living God. He possesses, along with others, the unshakable conviction that meaning, direction, and hope in life come not from within oneself but from the very Creator of all things. And this conviction—this indisputable sense of God's presence—is the ultimate basis for the Christian's faith and for what he says to his fellow men and women.

---

[1] Karl Barth, *Church Dogmatics: A Selection*, by Helmut Gollwitzer; G. W. Bromiley, trans. and ed. (New York: Harper & Row, Publishers, 1962), p. 65.

[2] The phrase is Richard Niebuhr's, from *The Meaning of Revelation* (New York: The Macmillan Company, 1941), p. 8.

[3] *Ibid.*, p. 141.

[4] Gordon Kaufman, *Systematic Theology: A Historicist Perspective* (New York: Charles Scribner's Sons, 1968), p. 21.

[5] John Macquarrie, *Principles of Christian Theology* (New York: Charles Scribner's Sons, 1966), p. 79.

[6] Pascal, *Pensées: The Provincial Letters*, W. F. Trotter, trans. (New York: The Modern Library, 1941), No. 430, p. 140.

Chapter 3

On Being Human: *What Are We Like and Where Are We Headed?* [1]

If the shameless fibbing of the cigarette hucksters and the barbarity of Hitler at Auschwitz and Buchenwald have anything in common, it is this: Both show that human beings are able to carry out villainies far more deliberate and malicious than anything we would ever expect from animals. But consider the devotion of a parent to a Mongoloid child or the decision of a society to do more for its aged and its poor. These illustrate the opposite, that human beings can live by an ideal far higher than that of any animal.

What is a human being? This is one of the principal questions of Christian faith, indeed, of the entire human race. And in trying to answer it, one of the most telling observations we ever make is that we differ from the animals in more than just the external sense of appearance.

We notice, for example, that while the animals are content with survival, we are not. When *we* try to subdue and enslave each other, it is often not simply because we want to preserve ourselves. *Our* crimes, commonly and often with careful premeditation, are committed to satisfy lusts or to seize power or to acquire wealth—whether or not there is any need on our part.

Then we notice that while the animals never rise above their survival instincts, we apparently do. On occasion, at least, human beings do live for others. What emerges from all this is the clear impression that our own inner lives are more complex than the survival impulse and that we are capable somehow of being a lot better or a lot worse than the animals. We are, in truth, moral beings.

Now Christianity has a particular view of man's life as a moral being, which I undertake to explain in the next few pages. Indeed, without such an explanation, much of what I am saying in this book would be so much clutter and hodgepodge. For in order to get a fully rounded sense of what Christian faith is about and of what God is doing in the world, it is necessary to know what Christians believe about our human existence.

Presupposed in all Christian talk on this subject is a certain idea about the makeup of human personality. First of all, a human being is someone who is conscious of being a self. We all know that we can think and act and feel. We know that we have some power to evaluate ourselves and some power to determine what we will do next. We can say, "I am mad at myself," or "I will get married in June," and these expressions actually mean something to us. We actually are aware of ourselves. We are able to make judgments about what we have done and decisions about what we are going to do.

In the second place, a human being is someone

who is conscious of certain limits on himself. We can see our situation. We know about ourselves and about our world, and it becomes clear to us that we are confined within certain boudaries. Life lasts only so long. We can achieve, given circumstances and our abilities, only so much.

But along with this awareness of our limitations we have the capacity to dream, to yearn for more than what we have. And severe uneasiness inside inevitably results. Knowing what we know, yet having our dreams of a better world, of higher achievement, and of some kind of deeper inner meaning, we cannot rest content.

Here religion gets into the picture, for in the state of discontent all of us reach out for some kind of hope. The dreams of our imagination, together with the frailty of our power to achieve those dreams, lead us all to choose some god, to place confidence in some ultimate center of meaning. I do not mean, obviously, that we all get into some kind of conventional, churchgoing religion. I just mean that we are all religious in the sense of having our own ultimate value—our own basis for hope and meaning. It may be very secular and atheistic, or it may be a narrow Bible-thumping fundamentalism, but it is still, in the broad sense of the word, our religion. We reject certain forms of religion, but never in practical life do we actually reject religion. We all cling to that which has final value and meaning for us. We all have our god.

The most decisive question which faces us is, of course, the question of which god to choose. If a person's god is, by definition, the very center or pivot of his life, then it follows that his god will determine how well and how meaningfully he lives. A person's god may give him inner peace, or it may reduce him to bitterness and inner turmoil.

How does the God whom Christians acknowledge affect human lives? What does He have to do with what we are here for and where we are going? And what does He have to do with the way we are?

In the first place, the Christian faith repudiates despair and pessimism. The Greek poet Empedocles wrote, "Alas, ye wretched, ye unblessed race of mortal beings, Of what strifes and of what groans were ye born."[2] When faced with that most compelling of riddles, the riddle of why we are here and of what we are doing on our spinning globe, Empedocles expressed defeat and hopelessness. He, as surely, I suppose, as anyone else, wanted to know if there was any enduring goodness in the world, any meaning, any ground for hope. Yet for him the answer was No. We are a wretched, unblessed race.

Not so, says the Christian faith. Despite the fact of evil and despite the seeming precariousness of our hopes and loves, we can say—no, shout!—a resounding Yes to human life. There *is* a basis for meaning. There *is* a ground for hope. There *is* a way to be at peace inside.

That we have been put here, not by rude chance, not by demons, but by a God of love and power, is the most fundamental of all Christian affirmations. The solitary individual is not a drying leaf buffeted by senseless winds, fated for nothingness. The solitary individual is somebody. He is crafted from the workbench of Divinity. He is free and capable of noble causes. As for the society at large, it too has been put here by a God of love and power. The world community is not a jungle of scrapping beasts destined for oblivion. It is a community whose life will be preserved, whose worth is inestimable, and whose destiny is peace and love.

In John 3:16, perhaps the best-known of all Biblical texts, Jesus began, "For God so loved the world . . ." Another time, quoting from the Old Testament, He said, " 'You shall love the Lord your God with all your heart' " (Matthew 22:37). He meant that love can exist betweeen a person and the very Maker of heaven and earth. So, far from Empedocles' vision of our race as wretched and unblessed, the Christian faith says we are meant not only to love one another but also to participate in a relationship of love with the Creator Himself.

When we sense disharmony between ourselves and Reality, we need not despair, for disharmony is not our unavoidable fate. God made us and intended us to enjoy a close connection with Himself. We are intended to be at one with the Source of life and thereby at one with ourselves. This vision of human destiny—sublime, astonishing, fertile with comfort and joy—is the vision of the Christian faith.

Yet, for all this trumpeting of good news about human destiny, the Christian cannot evade the plain fact that it is a harrowing experience to inhabit the earth. Evil, as Langdon Gilkey writes, "bestrides our existence like a conqueror."[3] What can be said of this? If God is good and if He created all things, why the broken hearts and wounded bodies?

It is impossible to get at the answer without first taking seriously the idea that there can be love and trust between people and their Maker. Human destiny, according to the Christian faith, is not mindless submission or the rigid obedience of a robot. Human destiny involves words such as *response* and *trust* and *love*. These words are drained of their meaning, and any "relationships" can be chalked up to the whims of a tyrant, unless God has given us the freedom to make real choices.

The happy truth, says the Christian faith, is that when God made us, He did not make a race of robots. Neither did He put us into an environment in which we could have no control of ourselves. One of the things Christians mean when they say God made a good world is that our world is not one in which the forces of nature or a brute cycle of cause and effect rob us of our moral powers. What we think and do is not an impersonal, automatic response to what goes on in our environment any more than it is something programmed by a cosmic tyrant.

God has made us free. We rise above our surroundings. We transcend the forces that act upon us. The decisions we make are really our decisions. If it were otherwise, not only Christian theology but all of philosophy and ethics as well would be a farce and a deception, and we would all be as characterless as mice.

Yet there is one trouble with human freedom. People can make the wrong choices and things can go bad. There was no way, short of meddling with free choice, for the Creator to ensure that His creatures would remain true to Him and thereby to the highest in themselves. Something akin to a police state would have been required to bring this about, but a police state would have left the whole idea of love and trust between God and people in a shambles.

Each day's newspaper makes it plain that when confronted with the terrible alternative of being loyal to God or to something less than God, we go sadly wrong much of the time. That is why a chapter on being human takes us, unavoidably, to the ugly and unpopular word *sin,* a word we would all rather forget. We come to a subject which, though unpleasant, is nonetheless pivotal.

It is commonplace, of course, to connect sin with sex or rule-breaking. But this caricature distorts instead of helps our understanding. Basically, sin has to do with relationships—with personal loyalties—and not with sex or the breaking of rules. According to the Bible, wrong choice causes all human troubles. The fatal error is exchanging "the truth about God for a lie" and of worshiping and serving "the creature rather than the Creator" (Romans 1:24, 25). When our deepest loyalties go not to the Creator Himself but to something the Creator has made, then we are involved in sin. And that is when things go bad.

This explains why it is a complete misunderstanding to think that sin is basically a matter of breaking rules. Whenever we look at sin this way, we trivialize it, reduce it to a mistake like the utterance of a swear word. But sin is more serious than that. Sin means a denial of faith in the Creator and a denial of our creaturely dependence upon Him for everything we have. Sin, in other words, is pride—the near-unspeakable enormity of saying God is someone we can do without.

The Bible puts it unmistakably: "For whatever does not proceed from faith [that is, from an attitude of absolute dependence on God] is sin" (Romans 14:23).

The unfortunate thing, of course, is that sin has dire consequences. When this pride, this lack of faith, starts to soften up the delicate architecture of human personality, some kind of collapse results. It is not a total collapse but nevertheless a tragic one, and that is why Paul wrote concerning sinners: "Claiming to be wise, they became fools" (Romans 1:22). Saying No to God is grotesque foolishness, for it inevitably brings upon us the ills we are so tired of having to face.

God intended in the creation that men and women should have a perfect love for Him and for one another. But we lose the freedom to have this perfect love when we sin. Once the self breaks with its Source, a massive disorder occurs. We are no longer able to have an "inmost disposition" of perfect love. We are no longer able to have complete control of ourselves. Not even the best of intentions nor even the most arduous self-discipline can bring total success in the command of our inner lives. Jesus brought this out unmistakably: " 'Every one who commits sin,' " He said, " 'is a slave to sin' " (John 8:34).

Yet this does not mean we have lost all ability to obey moral laws and commandments. Paul acknowledged that even among sinners there is conduct which can be described *legally* as either good or bad (see Romans 13:3). It is quite possible for the sinner to avoid murder, burglary, evasion of income tax, and the breaking of speed limits. It is even possible to obey the civil rights laws. But it is not possible *not* to be a sinner. It is not possible to have the perfect love—the perfect compassion and concern—that God requires and intends.

This explains the various forms of exploitation and selfishness familiar to us all. Even the best of men and women are not totally free from the inner itch to control and exploit. To some degree or other, all who are encumbered and weakened by sin go about seeking life at the expense of other life. And instead of the harmony of life with life that is the goal of all sensitive persons, there is indifference and rivalry and even violence.

A few paragraphs ago I said that sin and sex go together in people's minds. The idea has arisen that, for the Christian, sensual pleasure is something to be guilty about. Before proceeding to the next point in the chapter, I want to say clearly that this is anti-Biblical. Greek thinkers of the Hellenistic period thought evil was due to the life of the senses, and this idea infiltrated Christian thought early in the church's history. For a time the church seemed to put down the sexual aspect of human life, but the Bible corrects this mistake. Any insult against the body, any feeling that it is something to be ashamed of, contradicts Scripture. The Bible celebrates the physical—in the beginning God made sexuality—and its moral view is meant to preserve and enhance the physical. Scripture does deplore excessive or uncontrolled devotion to physical impulse and desire, but only because this kind of excess destroys what God created to be enjoyed.

Indeed, the whole trouble with sin in whatever form it may manifest itself is that it destroys what

God made to be enjoyed. It stifles and finally extinguishes life itself. If sin seems to hold out a certain promise—if it is somehow easy to fantasize about its supposed joys—in the end the whole business turns out to be a sad and tiresome fraud. That is one reason why Biblical writers and contemporary Christians denounce sin with such vehemence.

Now that I have said what sin is and what it does and that our *real* destiny is to enjoy relationships of love and trust with God and with each other, there remains an important, though difficult, matter to consider. We must examine two assertions that, on the face of it, seem incompatible with each other. The first is that everyone participates in the kind of pride I have spoken about, the pride that breaks down the relationship of human beings with God and with each other. (The Bible bluntly and simply declares in Romans 3:23 that "all have sinned.") The second is that it is not necessary to participate in sin. We are fully responsible for what we do. (Or, as Romans 1:20 says, "they are without excuse.")

The first assertion suggests that a fundamental defect afflicts the entire human race. This is a miserable thought, possibly as miserable as any that can be imagined. Yet even though our natural inclination is to remain optimistic about ourselves, our behavior and feelings regularly uphold the idea that something is terribly the matter. For example, doing the good thing is never easy for us; yet being evil-minded or indifferent is like coasting downhill. A sense of difficulty and of sacrifice goes along with helping the poor, but ignoring them is simple.

We also can gain insight into our sinfulness from the habit we have of extending ourselves to others only when we can reasonably expect to get something in return. If someone is in trouble whose respect we need or whose friendship we covet, we can be counted on to help him. If a race of people begins "getting out of hand," as blacks did when they lost their docility in the fifties and sixties, then finally we will get around to passing civil rights laws. If it is in our "national interest" to treat some foreign power decently, then we will be decent. We taint our ventures into brotherhood with the pigment of self-concern.

A final clue to our true nature is that even when we do perform some noble deed, it still ends up a venture of self-promotion. Jean-Baptiste Clamence, protagonist in Camus' *The Fall,* confesses, "When I was concerned with others, I was so out of pure condescension, in utter freedom, and all the credit went to me: my self-esteem would go up a degree."

Unless Christians are deceived, Clamence is all of us. And this, of course, is the problem. By giving ourselves the credit, we deny our dependence on God. We center our deepest trust and loyalty on ourselves and not on our Maker. And this fatal error perpetuates our troubles and our sense of restlessness, the feeling we share that somehow all is not well.

Yet, though sin is universal, it is not really necessary, according to Christianity. It is wrong to suppose that we cannot help ourselves. We are all responsible for what we do. If it is impossible to prove this, nonetheless certain signals in common human experience support the truthfulness of the Christian position.

One such signal is the fact that people hold each other responsible. The idea that we are free to choose and that we ought to be held accountable for what we think and do is something on which there is universal, or near-universal, agreement. If a high-ranking executive is found embezzling company money, he is imprisoned. If a race of people brutally suppresses another race of people, thoughtful individuals commonly assume that the offending race is somehow responsible for what has happened.

Our responsibility is further attested by the personal feelings of remorse that follow evil action. People *feel* responsible. They know what guilt is. Christians take this universal experience of guilt as evidence that the evil of our lives is very much our fault. We can never load off all the blame onto something besides ourselves.

I have said before that evil action follows from the prior evil of making a god out of something that is not God at all. My point here, in recalling this, is that the remorse we all feel is ultimately more than a sense of our immoral conduct. According to Christianity, all of us—whether or not we have an explicit knowledge of God—sense that something is the matter with our worship of ourselves. We all sense that glorification of our finite selves somehow puts us at odds with Reality, somehow is the cause of our troubles and the ultimate source of the uneasy conscience common to us all. So we not only are responsible for our immoral conduct but are responsible—indeed, "without excuse"—for the sin we commit against God Himself.

As we have seen in this chapter, the astonishing potential and ability with which God created us carried with them astonishing risks. When He made us with the capacity to decide for ourselves about life's most awesome questions—questions about loyalty and love and faith—there arose the possibility that we would make wrong decisions. And that is what we have been doing. As a result, the human predicament has descended on us all. We all know the face of evil, because it confronts us every day.

I would be amiss, of course, to obscure the fact that although much of the evil in the world can be explained as a result of the misuse of human freedom, some cannot be so explained. No Christian can produce a completely satisfying explanation of how a good God could preside over a world in which floods, famines, and other natural evils bring indiscriminate pain and slaughter to millions. Indeed, the only way to give a completely logical and consistent account of these so-called natural evils is to concede that they are built into the very structure of our existence.

Yet on this point Christianity steadfastly disagrees with other major philosophical accounts of the universe. The Christian believes that evil is "a *perversion* rather than a *necessity* of our existence."[4] Neither the pain of natural evil nor the pain of human sin is the last word in our lives. Those philosophies which are more consistent provide no firm basis for hope. Christianity does provide a basis for hope, for Christianity says evil can be removed.

How? Through the love and concern of the Creator Himself. The Christian believes that God has moved, in love and utter decisiveness, to repair the damage that has been done in His world. Throughout the rest of the book we will hear more about the process of repair. The first step will be to ask about Jesus Christ, the central figure of the Christian faith.

---

[1]Throughout this chapter I am heavily indebted to Reinhold Niebuhr's *The Nature and Destiny of Man*, Vol. I.

[2]Quoted in *Maker of Heaven and Earth*, by Langdon Gilkey (New York: Doubleday & Company, Inc., 1959), p. 156.

[3]*Ibid.*, p. 178.

[4]*Ibid.*, p. 182.

Chapter 4

Jesus Christ: *God's Kingdom Arrives*

That in the years after a man's death there should spring up a community professing allegiance to him as their *living* Lord seems as improbable as a clap of thunder from a cloudless sky. Even so, that is what happened following the death of Jesus of Nazareth.

Only a couple of references by secular historians attest the fact that He ever lived. Otherwise the only reports we have about Jesus were written by members of the believing religious community—the early church. They express this community's inspired understanding of His significance for mankind and disclose its memory of His life and of the historical events surrounding it. What these early documents—enshrined in our New Testament—have to tell is, quite simply, astonishing.

Among them are the Four Gospels, which narrate Jesus' life; or rather, they embody the beliefs of the earliest Christians about Jesus. Not biographies in the modern sense, they omit most details. We know nothing of Jesus' early childhood or His young manhood. Instead, they focus on a few incidents and sayings.

Only the facts worth remembering—that is, the facts considered to have utmost significance for men and women everywhere—were written down. The men who gave us the Gospels were not scholars so much as witnesses bearing testimony to what they had seen and heard.

Among the great themes they put forth is this: After His baptism Jesus of Nazareth began "preaching the gospel of God, and saying, 'The time is fulfilled, and the kingdom of God is at hand: repent, and believe in the gospel' " (Mark 1:14, 15). I will say more about "the kingdom of God" in the last chapter of the book. It is enough for the moment to state that Jesus meant that God Himself was now making a decisive impact on human affairs. God Himself was *doing something great*—something toward which the Hebrew people had looked for centuries. He was changing things. He was inaugurating a new age. It was crucial, therefore, that people own up to their self-centeredness, turn from it, and have faith in God.

The amazing part was this: Jesus *identified Himself* with what was happening. And He did not do so in a casual way as though He were just a member of God's staff come to make an announcement. He claimed that He Himself *was* the arrival of the kingdom. He Himself was changing things. The Pharisees asked Him once when the kingdom would come, and He said, " 'For behold, the kingdom of God is in the midst of you' " (Luke 17:21). The kingdom had already arrived, and the reason for saying so was that He was standing among them.

Jesus was on the earth, which meant God was doing

something great, something decisive. But this was the mere beginning. Jesus declared concerning the kingdom: " 'It is like a grain of mustard seed, which, when sown upon the ground, is the smallest of all the seeds on earth; yet when it is sown it grows up and becomes the greatest of all shrubs' " (Mark 4:31, 32). Although the kingdom had started small, it would end in a stupendous climax.

All through His ministry, Jesus' language about Himself suggested immense authority. He startled everyone by stating, " 'No one knows the Son except the Father, and no one knows the Father except the Son' " (Matthew 11:27). His words implied a unique oneness with God. It was just as startling when, concerning those who do not do the will of God, He said, " 'And then will I declare to them, "I never knew you; depart from me, you evildoers" ' " (Matthew 7:23). He assumed for Himself the right to pronounce final judgment on everyone.

The early church could not forget these things, nor could it forget His claim to mastery over the powers of evil. Of His ability to cast out devils, He said, " 'But no one can enter a strong man's house and plunder his goods, unless he first binds the strong man' " (Mark 3:27). Jesus even remarked that it was in His power to forgive sins, and as the scribes said, " 'Who can forgive sins but God alone?' " (Mark 2:7).

Three and one-half years after His first public appearances, Jesus was crucified. His death was a bitter surprise. Even so, there grew up afterward a body of believers affirming that what He had said about the significance of His mission was actually true. People began, in a word, to have faith in Jesus Christ. The work of the New Testament scholars has helped clarify what the essentials of that faith were.

When Paul wrote to the Corinthians for the first time, he reminded them of how he had preached to them at the start: "For I delivered to you as of first importance what I also received, that Christ died for our sins in accordance with the scriptures, that he was buried, that he was raised on the third day in accordance with the scriptures, and that he appeared to Cephas, then to the twelve" (1 Corinthians 15:3-5). Scholarship shows that Paul was quoting here a common confession of faith dating back to within the first decade after Jesus' death—some say to within the first five years.[1] If so, Paul's words represent the very early convictions of the church concerning Jesus Christ. He had died. He had been raised to life. And He was, therefore, Lord.

These convictions persisted beyond the first decade of the church's history. Paul wrote of them in the third decade after the Crucifixion, and they appear throughout his letters. Luke's account of early church history, The Acts of the Apostles, was written about a decade later than the first of Paul's letters. The early Christian sermons he included are samples of the kind of preaching that went on in Jerusalem from the beginning of Christianity, and they are certainly typical also of the preaching of Luke's day. And he, too, emphasized Jesus' death and resurrection and the church's evaluation of Him as Lord. He stressed the necessity that people turn from evil and seek forgiveness.

An obvious question arises: Why would anyone of

sound mind believe such things about the Man who, in the end, suffered public contempt and died as a common criminal? What accounts for the fact that this Man became the object of religious faith for a large community of people?

Jesus claimed, as I have said, to have immense authority. But that in itself could not have been the basis of faith; He may have been a lunatic. There had to be some confirmation of His claims, some evidence that He was not a charismatic fool. And there was. It came in His appearances after the Crucifixion. Though He had died, the tomb had not contained Him. Contrary to what they expected, the disciples saw and talked with Him, as the Gospels proclaim. And Paul wrote that He once "appeared to more than five hundred brethren at one time, most of whom are still alive" (1 Corinthians 15:6).

Jesus did not become the object of religious faith because of any speculative, intellectual theory. That is not what the early church based its theology upon. It was based, instead, upon an event, upon something that had happened. Hence, when the religious authorities instructed Peter and John to keep quiet concerning Jesus, they refused, saying they could not help but speak of what they had "seen and heard" (Acts 4:20).

But this in itself is not a satisfactory explanation. I can well imagine that the appearance of a man once dead would cause a great furor and excitement among those connected with it. I can also imagine that as the years and decades passed, the memory would fade until it became a mere oddity to be repeated for grandchildren and those with a taste for novelty. Why did this not happen in the case of the appearances of Jesus? Why didn't the memory fade?

The early believers did not speak of the Resurrection only. They also testified that Jesus Christ had made the difference in their lives. The first believers confessed faith in Jesus Christ because He had done something for them. He had been raised from the dead. They were certain of that. But more than that, He had affected them at the deepest levels of being. They found that once they accepted His invitation to faith, He freed them of guilt, and, full of inner security, they could confidently face the future. They had something compelling and urgent to live for. They had a mission and a hope, and that was everything.

Through commitment of the whole life to Jesus Christ, the early believers became certain that He really had initiated the kingdom of God. The Resurrection had been neither a prank of nature (without significance) nor an elaborate hoax. Jesus' message of freedom and hope was true. Their own experience had confirmed it. He really was their living Lord. And if He was Lord, if He was the One who could usher in the kingdom—the One who could do all these things for them—then . . . then Jesus Christ was God Himself!

But the first believers also remembered that Jesus had lived the life of a man and had actually died under Pontius Pilate. So they began to see that something utterly without parallel had happened: God had revealed Himself in a man. John wrote in his Gospel: "In the beginning was the Word, and the Word was with God, and the Word was God. . . . And the Word became flesh and dwelt among us" (John 1:1-14). Since there had existed in man's actual history One in whom God Himself was personally present and active, this became the central theme of the church's preaching and of the New Testament.

Now we come to the question, What is really meant by the Christian affirmation that God became man? Scottish theologian D. M. Baillie has put the answer this way: In Jesus Christ we must "reckon with a life that was wholly human and wholly divine, neither side limiting the other at all."[2]

Theologians call God's becoming a man the Incarnation. Since the concept affords a warehouse of possibility for confusion, it is well right away to say something of what Christians do *not* mean by the Incarnation. They do not mean that Jesus was God instead of man, that He was an intermediate type between God and man, or that Jesus' body was just a place where God took up temporary residence. Nor do they mean that Jesus was a human body with a divine mind or that He was a good man who got promoted to the level of God or that God changed into a man or that Jesus just seemed like a man but was not really a man.

None of these reflect what the Bible means to convey, though each was at one time or another widely propagated and subsequently renounced by the church. Historic Christianity asserts, quite unambiguously, that Jesus Christ was actually a man and, at the same time, actually God Himself.

On the one hand, this means that Jesus Christ reveals God Himself. If you want to understand God, the best place to go is to Jesus Christ, because what He did is what God did. Paul wrote, "God was in Christ reconciling the world to himself." But in the same context he said, "All this is from God" (2 Corinthians 5:18, 19).

If Jesus Christ was actually God Himself, He tells us what God is like. The best news to be derived from this is that God is not remote and disinterested but willing to take action on behalf of people who need help. He is neither too busy to go out of the way, nor does He have to be coaxed or placated before He will get involved. He goes to a world in trouble on His own initiative, seeking His creatures even before they seek Him.

More than this, Jesus shows that God will go the whole way, even to the point of personal suffering, in order to make things right again. Christians were, and still are, astonished to be worshiping Someone who was Himself willing to bear the terrible cost of human evil. (This is a topic of its own and is considered at length in the next chapter.) I do not know, of course, how to account for God's suffering, but to say otherwise—to say that only the human Jesus suffered—would turn the Incarnation into an empty bit of theatrics. To say that Jesus suffered is to say that God suffered.

The other side of the Incarnation is this: The humanity of Jesus was a genuine humanity. In the words of Scripture: He was "like his brethren in every respect" (Hebrews 2:17). He had a body, mind, and will and had to confront disappointments and struggles as other men do. He faced temptations as real, agonizing, and difficult as those of any human being. He faced the death that others must ultimately face. The One who could rescue the members of a lost race had to know what it is really like to be a man. Jesus knew. He had no special world to live in.

There was a key difference, though, between Him and others of our race. He was "one who in every respect had been tempted as we are, yet without sinning" (Hebrews 4:15). He achieved a life wholly committed to the Father. And according to Christianity, the achievement was based on an experience of faith of the kind that is available to anyone. Jesus had faith in the God who actually heard Him and helped Him in the same way that He actually hears and helps other human beings.

This means that even as Jesus tells us what God is like, He tells us what we are like, or rather, what we can be like. He is the complete definition of what it means to be a human being. He shows us that the truly real person is the one who has faith in God. He is the one who is absolutely for God instead of for himself and in that way absolutely for others instead of for himself.

Just how Jesus was truly God and truly man I cannot explain. Even the New Testament considered this a topic on which silence was the safest eloquence. As we have seen, the first believers came to their conclusions about Jesus not by logic or theorizing but by virtue of what they had seen and heard and what had been done at the deepest levels of their being.

How, then, does today's Christian come to his conclusions about Jesus? He does it in a way not dissimilar to that of his predecessors. Though I, for example, have not witnessed the appearances of Jesus, I firmly believe that they took place.

It is not, by the way, simpleminded in view of natural science to have this belief. Natural science only expresses the general validity of the laws of nature. It does not make final pronouncements on the possibility or impossibility of individual events. Natural science does not say that a resurrection from death is an impossibility; it only says that it is extremely improbable.

Concerning the appearances of Jesus, there is, in fact, good historical evidence that they occurred. The books of the New Testament were written, of course, from two to six decades after Jesus' death. But at least one of the early church's confessions of faith dates back, as I told you earlier, to within perhaps five years of His death. This is evidence available to any historian, whether or not he is sympathetic to the Christian religion. It attests that five years or so after the Crucifixion an actual community already affirmed the reality of the Resurrection. Considering how long ago the event occurred, this means that by normal standards of scholarship there is good historical foundation for calling the Resurrection a fact.[3]

But this alone does not explain my faith or that of any contemporary Christian. The first Christians did not speak of the Resurrection only. They said that Jesus had made the difference in their lives. The same is true for Christians now. Jesus' message of freedom and hope is confirmed *today* in the personal and collective experience of those who believe, and this, ultimately, explains the Christian's belief that the man Jesus of Nazareth was God Himself.

If an astronaut goes to the moon, you can give a

satisfactory rational explanation of what occurred. If God comes to the earth, you cannot. But if His coming makes it possible for millions to move from an artificial and troubled existence to a life of worth and fulfillment, it is something to shout about even though it is hard to understand. That is what believers have done from the beginning, and it is what they continue to do.

---

[1] See Wolfhart Pannenberg, *Jesus—God and Man* (Philadelphia: The Westminster Press, 1968), p. 90.

[2] D. M. Baillie, *God Was in Christ* (New York: Charles Scribner's Sons, 1948), p. 93.

[3] An extended argument along this line appears in *Jesus—God and Man*.

Chapter 5

Atonement:
Getting Back Together Again

In a tender and vivid scene from Dostoevski's masterpiece, *The Brothers Karamazov,* Father Zossima meets a group of peasant women who are crowded at the foot of the monastery portico. One woman who has been gazing at him in silence finally catches the Father's eye, and he asks: " 'What is it, my child?' " " 'I have sinned, Father,' " she says. " 'I am afraid of my sin.' "[1]

Anyone who thinks her sentiment is morbid eccentricity—that she would not have felt this way apart from conditioning by the church—would do well to consider that sin and guilt have been emphatic themes in literature where Christianity was unknown. The Greek poet Sophocles, writing more than four centuries before Christ, knew very well the feelings of the peasant woman. In his great tragedy *Antigone,* the tyrant of Thebes, seeing that his policies have led to the suicide first of Antigone and then of his own son, cries out: "Woe for the sins of a darkened soul, stubborn sins, fraught with death! . . . Woe is me, for the wretched blindness of my counsels."[2]

The shadow that haunted the peasant woman and the tyrant of Thebes has been the unwelcome companion of men and women throughout the ages. That something dreadful is the matter, that there is strident disharmony between what we are and what we should be, is the regular and unavoidable message of human conscience. The poet Dante spoke for everyone when he cried out, " 'O human race, born to fly upward, wherefore at a little wind dost thou so fall?' "[3]

What can be done? The contradiction between the destiny we were born for and the reality of our everyday lives is more than petty information like Babe Ruth's home-run record. It affects our whole being and outlook. It is a source of excruciating moral pain, and if the literature of the world is any witness, we all want desperately to be delivered from it. How can the disharmony in our lives be resolved? How can the moral anguish be relieved?

In the course of history, the problem has been dealt with in a number of ways, many of them starting from the assumption that people, by their own initiative, can draw themselves to the attention of the gods, find favor, and be granted peace. Whether your gods are divine powers or high ideals, this idea says that by your own power you can get into harmony with them, into accord with whatever it is that makes you feel guilty about your sins and afraid of death.

In some primitive religions, for example, people have tried to find peace by sacrificing their possessions—even their children—to the gods. This approach tries to strike a bargain with Heaven, hoping that the wrath of the gods will thereby be appeased and human unworthiness canceled out. It is an effort to buy off the forces that control destiny, to exchange sacrifices in return for the goodwill of the divine.

Such crude transactions between people and Heaven, of course, seem barbarous and repulsive in the modern world. But that does not mean we have abandoned the assumption behind them. In modern, secular society, many people still believe they can relieve themselves of moral anguish on their own initiative and power. Instead of crude sacrificing, the secular approach is that of moral endeavor. Many try to find peace through good behavior. What matters is not religious ritual but the condition of the heart. If you are a truly good person, committed to noble human ideals, your sense of moral anguish will be gone.

But there are troubles here. The first is that such an approach fails to deal with pain resulting from evils committed in the past. It is doubtful that all the good intentions in paradise could have saved the tyrant of Thebes from anguish over the two suicides for which he was to blame. And the second trouble I will mention is even more serious. Existentialist Albert Camus, in his novel *The Fall,* said as clearly as anyone what it is. Our ego is so unremitting an influence on our lives that we never produce a consistent inner goodness. The taint of selfishness compromises our noblest acts. And so the person who tries moralism, if he is sensitive at all, will see sooner or later that there is a residue of evil inside him that even his best efforts cannot remove completely.

Many people (some of them Christians) try yet another and final ploy. They adopt an attitude of utter self-abasement. If you are not good enough to get straight with Heaven, goes this kind of reasoning, try to be humble enough. Admit how despicable you are, and hope the divine powers give you a break for being honest.

But there is a flaw even here. The philosopher Nietzsche put it well when he said, " 'He who despises himself feels at the same time a certain respect for himself as being a despiser of himself.' "[4] In other words, the person who tries self-abasement inevitably becomes proud of his humility. And he brings it to his gods as a kind of evidence that he is all right, presuming that now they will remove the moral pain and replace it with peace of mind.

This represents once again, however, an effort to work out a deal with the divine powers. It assumes that a person can sit down and negotiate a settlement with Heaven itself. The same assumption is at work as the one that lies behind primitive, sacrificial religion, namely, that people on their own initiative and power can relieve themselves of moral anguish and get into a positive relationship with the divine.

Just now we have come to a point where we can see very clearly how Christianity fundamentally differs in its way of dealing with this problem. For it is precisely the assumption I am talking about—and the various approaches that are based upon it—that Christianity says will never, never do. In the Christian view of things, efforts to find peace that begin with human initiative and human power do not produce peace at all but only greater and greater anguish. Such efforts do not take care of sin, because—and this is the key point—*they are themselves sinful.*

I explained in an earlier chapter that the beginning of sin—and the womb from which all moral evils arise—is the attempt by men and women to be on a par with God, to be His equal. And just when a person thinks he can negotiate with God, just when he thinks something he has done will lead to a settlement, he has attempted to be God's equal. That is why the person who tries to deal with sin in his own way and by his own power gets anguish instead of peace. The method leads him straight back to the sin with which he began, straight back to the terrible sense of disharmony between himself and the destiny for which he was born.

So we return to the same momentous question: How *is* the disharmony in our lives to be resolved? The answer of Christian faith, unlike these other answers, is that God does it. Where we fail, He succeeds. Even though we have all gone wrong, we are not handcuffed to our moral anguish. God Himself has stepped in and made peace of mind a true possibility. God Himself is our liberator.

We have come now to the Christian doctrine of the Atonement, or, in plain talk, the Christian view of how to get rid of sin and of how to be at one with God again and at one with self. Christians believe that because of what God Himself has done, we can cease being afraid of our sins. And when we are not afraid of our sins, when we are at one with our Maker, there is nothing whatever to be afraid of. Neither death, famine, tyranny, cancer, nor anything else can make us shiver with cowardice and fright. Even though evil remains painful and our existence difficult, nothing can ultimately devastate our lives. The sting of evil—even the sting of death—is gone. We are in God's good hands. *Because of what He has done, we can live with inner serenity and joy.*

This bit of good news is, in essence, what the doctrine of the Atonement is about. Yet there is more, of course, to be said, more explanation of what God has done and why, and for this we must go back to the beginning. We must remember that at Creation God did not put together a population of robots who would obey Him by a kind of bloodless, mechanical instinct. Instead, He made a people free to live in peaceable relations with their Maker—or free to resist their Maker's will. And as the Biblical story of the Fall makes clear, every one of us has resisted His will. We are all in one way or another pretenders to His throne. We are all trying to set ourselves up as gods instead of trusting the real God who made us. We all participate in the revolt against the Creator.

How evil got started—particularly evils such as famine and earthquake—is in the end a mystery too deep for words. Even so, from Old Testament times the believing community has been certain that evil and revolt against God somehow go together. Because of human resistance to God's will, the world has fallen into difficult times.

And yet there is a paradox here. While it is *our* resistance that gets us into trouble, the grip of evil is so strong it is reasonable to say that a hostile power, a raging tyrant, is in our midst. The Bible writers speak of "the ruler of this world," of "the evil one," of "the devil" and "Satan," or in the plural, of "principalities and powers" (John 12:31; 1 John 5:19; 1 John 3:8; Job 1:6; Colossians 2:15). Indeed, there is a full-blown cosmic warfare in progress, with these evil persons arrayed not only against us but against the Creator Himself. This is the Bible's way of saying very clearly that wickedness and pain have a dread, mysterious clutch upon our lives. Even though we sense a responsibility for our sin, at the same time evil comes upon us from without, like an enemy.

But now consider the central truth of the gospel and of all Christian talk about at-one-ment or Atonement. *God has already defeated the enemy.* How can we overcome the tyranny of evil? How can we be comfortable again with ourselves and God? The answer is that God, and God alone, can overcome the tyrants. God, and God alone, can create conditions in which we can be comfortable again with ourselves and Him. And He has done these things already.

The story of how God defeated the enemy is surely the most splendid paradox you will ever come across. For He did not horsewhip anyone, begin guerrilla warfare, or issue intimidating threats. Instead, He defeated the enemy by an act of powerlessness, by dying at the cross. The testimony of the first believers is that Jesus Christ, the Son of God, "freed us from our sins by his blood" (Revelation 1:5).

Here is a great mystery, of course. Just why this particular death was crucial or just how it worked is something not even the New Testament writers undertake to explain. The how of the cross, for them as for us, is a puzzle. But the what of the cross—the fact that this one death has put the world into a new relationship with the divine—is a matter of certainty. The New Testament writers, like all the Christians who have followed them, are absolutely sure that things are better now because a fundamental change has occurred.

What sort of change? To begin, consider Dostoevski's peasant woman. Her anguish lay in the sense she had of the evil in her own heart. How could she be at peace with God if her life did not measure up to Heaven's perfect laws? For her (and for all of us who are less than what we should be) Christianity makes a very simple and beautiful announcement: Guilt does not have to devastate us anymore. Even though our moral lives are flawed, we can be at peace with our Maker. "Christ [has] redeemed us from the curse of the law" (Galatians 3:13).

Paul wrote those words, and they are as welcome as a first love. They mean that the relation between us and God is not decided by how good *we* are. Though the laws of Heaven are perfect—condemning everything from tyranny to the plain old nastiness by which we make others miserable—this does not put some eternal curse upon us. The divine policy of love was ratified, so to speak, at the cross. And this means that God can embrace us, can call us His own, even if we have been tainted with racism or sexism, even if we have robbed banks or committed rape. If in any way we are condemned by the law, by the contradiction between what we are and what we were born for, He can show mercy to us and forgive us. We need not be guilt-ridden, and we need not be afraid.

But people who are afraid of their sins because they

feel condemned by them also cower before the prospect of the evil and horror to which sins lead. And this brings us to another meaning of the Christian doctrine of the Atonement. Said John, "The reason the Son of God appeared was to destroy the works of the devil" (1 John 3:8). The language here is unmistakable. Thanks to the cross and the events surrounding it, God is the victor over the powers of evil in our world. His love—and not a bomb, a tyranny, or a natural disaster—will be the final word in the universe. Even death, the "last enemy," "is swallowed up in victory" (1 Corinthians 15:26, 54).

There is, in short, a new relation between the world and God. God has broken down the system of merit so that despite our unacceptability we can be accepted. And He has triumphed over the powers of evil so that despite our pain and suffering we can move toward the future with confidence and hope. Through His initiative, we are saved.

It is just here, however, that we run up against Biblical language that causes bewilderment or even contempt for the gospel in the modern mind. I mean the language of blood sacrifice. According to the New Testament, we are saved by the blood of Jesus Christ (see Romans 5:9). We are delivered from evil "not with perishable things such as silver or gold, but with the precious blood of Christ, like that of a lamb without blemish or spot" (1 Peter 1:18, 19). Jesus died, according to the New Testament, for our sake and in our stead (see, for example, John 13:37; Romans 5:8).

This has suggested to some the idea that Jesus' death was a vicarious punishment demanded by a cruel heavenly tyrant. The picture here is of a God who is full of vindictive anger, a God who, if sinners are to go free, demands at least that an innocent victim suffer and die in their place. Quite understandably, this kind of ugly and volatile God offends sensitive persons. A religion putting forward such a God and such an atonement would surely be immoral and unsupportable.

Happily, however, the idea of penal substitution—of Jesus as God's luckless scapegoat—is not New Testament doctrine but a distortion of it. While the cross was necessary, fulfilling the divine (though to us mysterious) purpose, it was not a punishment. It was not a martyrdom required to pacify a temperamental deity. On the contrary, it was God Himself—not someone picked upon by Him—who underwent the suffering of the cross.

In the history of Christianity there have been at least three classic attempts to explain why the cross was necessary. One group of theologians has said Christ's sacrifice occurred because of an arbitrary decree from Heaven. Another group has argued that the cross was necessary to satisfy the divine standard of justice. Yet another group has said Christ had to die in order to satisfy *our* moral sense, in order, as it were, to make God's justice believable to us.

But "the crucial point is that none of these theological standpoints allows you to think of God as a cruel tyrant exacting his due from an innocent Person in our behalf."[5] The classic thinkers of the church have all agreed, with Scripture, that God Himself "became flesh and dwelt among us" (John 1:14). The offended

One Himself identified completely with our race, bore our guilt as if it were His own, and suffered on our behalf. It was *His* action—not someone else's—that defeated the tyrants and opened the way for a new togetherness, a new unity between God and humanity.

One other point, equally important, must be made before the chapter ends. If human response to God's initiative is No, there can be no Atonement, no experience of togetherness. Unless a person is willing to identify with God, he cannot benefit from what God has done on his behalf.

The Hebrew system of sacrifice, outlined in the Old Testament yet only vaguely familiar to most people, vividly illustrates this truth. In the rituals of the ancient Hebrews, which to many moderns seem quaint and confusing, the individual brought an animal victim with him to the altar at the sanctuary or temple. The victim was slain and offered as a burnt offering.

But the point of this was not vicarious punishment, as though the victim were paying the penalty while the sinner went free. The point, symbolized before the slaying when the individual laid his hands on the victim's head, was to show that spiritually the individual was one with the victim. The whole ceremony represented the individual's surrender of his life to the God who, by suffering, delivers His people.

English theologian J. S. Whale says that "Christianity brings man to God by bringing God to man."[6] It is a clever epigram, and true. But even after God has come to man, togetherness can be foiled. Instead of saying, with Paul, "I am crucified with Christ" (Galatians 2:20), a person can refuse to identify with the God who suffers on his behalf. For him, God's work of atonement has been in vain.

But that does not dim the magnificence of what God has done. It does not threaten the other possibility envisioned by the Christian faith. God, in Jesus Christ, appeared on the earth, and suffered and died. Why? Irenaeus, one of the early fathers of the church, said it all: " 'That He might destroy sin, overcome death, and give life to man.' "[7]

---

[1]*Britannica Great Books,* Vol. 52, p. 24.

[2]*Ibid.,* Vol. 5, p. 141.

[3]*Ibid.,* Vol. 21, p. 71.

[4]Quoted in J. S. Whale, *Christian Doctrine* (Cambridge: Cambridge University Press, 1961), p. 76. I am considerably indebted to Whale in this chapter.

[5]*Ibid.,* p. 93.

[6]*Ibid.,* p. 79.

[7]Quoted in Gustaf Aulen, *Christus Victor* (New York: The Macmillan Company, 1961), p. 19.

Chapter 6

Christian Morals:
A New Kind of Loving

By now it should surprise no one that when we take up the subject of Christian morals we must begin with Jesus Christ. That bit of Christianity which tells us how we ought to relate to people and to society is like all the other bits. It takes us right back to Palestine and the story of an ex-carpenter from Nazareth.

The first clue to our subject is put well by Langdon Gilkey, who writes, "This is ethically what being a Christian is, namely to understand Jesus Christ to be the only clear clue to the Father's will for us."[1] He means that if we want to learn what Christian morals are all about, we do so by reflecting on the God of Christian faith and on His self-revelation in the person of Jesus Christ. The chapter that just ended, for example, provides a key to the one we are just beginning. We learned that Christ's mission was to reunite the separated. He established a new relation between God and the world. He created the conditions whereby God and human beings could be at one again and could enjoy a new togetherness.

This points to *our* mission, for the purpose of Christian morals is to bring people together again. A new relation among men and women, a new togetherness in society, is the unmistakable aim of all truly Christian endeavor.

Already a question arises. If togetherness is the aim, *how* is it achieved? What we have already learned about Jesus Christ offers a clue to the answer. *We are to care as He cared—abandoning personal acquisitiveness and seeking the good of others no matter what the circumstance.*

There is a word that describes what Christ has done for us, and it is the basis for all that can be said about Christian morals. It is *agapē,* a Greek word meaning love. But love that goes by the name *agapē* is not like the frivolous twentieth-century variety you hear about in pop tunes or soap operas. It is not a pleasing emotional mist, and it is not based on mood or inclination. It is not the same as liking or having a good feeling about something or someone. *Agapē* means, quite simply, a concern for your neighbor whether he is attractive or not. It means caring for the unloved and unknown as well as for the loved and known. It means goodwill for the adversary as well as for the ally. Kierkegaard called it the "eternal equality in loving."[2]

The basis for this radical idea of love is God's love, for it is precisely God's nature to shower His care upon all, even if they are unlikable or do not "deserve" sympathy. The essence of the gospel story is that God acts on behalf of people who have turned against Him. He loves all without restriction. He loves all in spite of their bad, or even monstrous, qualities. And just this kind of love bears the name *agapē.* It means, as William Barclay has written, "an undefeatable attitude of goodwill; it means that no matter what the other man does to us we will never under any circumstances seek anything but his good."[3]

If Jesus Christ is the only unmistakable clue to the Father's will for us, this says something else about *agapē*. It is a love that takes the initiative. Some Christians isolate themselves from pain and suffering to avoid risks, to be prudent in guarding their own safety and satisfaction. But such a detached existence is irrelevant and cowardly—just the opposite of what God demands. Going into the world, sacrificing for it, even dying for it—this is what the gospel demands. If God Himself could do this for a stricken—and in many ways despicable—society, then that is what men and women must do.

I said in the title of the chapter that all this represents a new kind of loving. It was new, of course, to the ancient world—a shockingly different concept both to the Jews and the Greeks. But *agapē* is new even today—in that it is unexpected. To the natural eye *agapē* seems strange, unrealistic, and contrary to good sense. It seems reasonable to act toward others in a way that will make them act considerately toward you or to be kind to those who are kind to you. But if goodwill should require self-sacrifice—and the other person or group is riffraff anyway, not contributing a fair share of effort or kindness—then it is smart to pull back. It's a dog-eat-dog world. Why go out of the way?

Despite such good sense, however, the Christian faith argues for the kind of love God demonstrated at the cross. And not without reason, for the grave flaw in approaching things sensibly is this: If your concern for others depends on whether they respond in the way you want them to, your efforts are inevitably compromised by the fear that they will not do so. Your whole moral life becomes a kind of tit-for-tat game—if you do this I'll do that—and the quest for a new relation among people dies on a cross of fear and caution.

Jesus asked, " 'For if you love those who love you, what reward have you? Do not even the tax collectors do the same?' " (Matthew 5:46, RSV). Christians take (or should take) this warning with great seriousness. For if you (or your company or government) operate purely from the standpoint of your own advantage—loving only when love is safe and pleasant—no real risks are taken and no genuinely new achievements of brotherhood can occur.

You would not, for example, expect an employer who thinks primarily of himself to hire an ex-convict, except perhaps as an act of self-serving public relations. Statistically it is no doubt safer to hire people who have not had run-ins with the law. But the safe course does nothing to improve relations between the privileged elite whom the employer may represent and the troubled, less-privileged persons whom the ex-convict may represent. Brotherhood dies on a cross of caution.

Or again, you cannot expect a rich government concerned only for the national self-interest to do any more for the poor nations than is necessary to maintain a semblance of peace. If this can be done while millions starve and the rich continue to hoard their resources, then true brotherhood in the world can be blithely and purposefully postponed.

Now there is no mistaking what all this means for the individual. (What it means for governments is more complex, but it certainly means that concern *only* for the national self-interest is wrong.) The individual, if he would achieve genuine moral success, must be willing to minimize—in unusual circumstances, even ignore—his own good fortune on the earth. So in one way the Christian must concede a debating point to his opponents: The Christian ethic cannot be justified in purely this-worldly terms. Saying a person should risk hurt to himself, perhaps even death, in order to help the hostile or undeserving, will certainly not win converts among those who believe that once this life ends, everything is over. From that perspective, the risk in Christian love seems dubious indeed.

This takes us to the indispensable tie between the morals of the Christian and the faith of the Christian. When a lawyer asked Jesus which was the great commandment in the law, Jesus replied, " 'You shall love the Lord your God with all your heart, and with all your soul, and with all your mind. This is the great and first commandment. And a second is like it. You shall love your neighbor as yourself' " (Matthew 5:37-39, RSV). What is pertinent here is that, for Jesus, a relationship of faith and love with God is more important than anything else. Your relationship with your neighbor comes second. And, surprisingly, this is not pious humbug. It does not undercut the significance of relationships in the here and now as though they had second-rate importance. It says instead—a shrewd point, indeed—that without faith the whole structure of self-giving love loses its necessary foundation and crumbles into pieces.

It is easy, when you think about it, to see why this is the case. Without assurance that you are in the hands of a loving and powerful God, the survival impulse—no boon to moral courage—begins to take over the life. If you are an employer, it begins to make good sense to stay away from the ex-convict. He's made his bed. Let him lie in it. Survival is the name of the game, and don't take unnecessary risks if you know what's good for you.

But faith makes possible unnecessary risks. Paul wrote, "If we live, we live to the Lord, and if we die, we die to the Lord; so then, whether we live or whether we die, we are the Lord's" (Romans 14:8, RSV). The conviction that nothing whatever can separate us permanently from God provides a certain—not flimsy or unsure—basis for self-giving love. It gives the strength to dare, to take risks for brotherhood and sisterhood.

We have learned, up to now, something of what *agapē* is and of how its necessary foundation involves trust in God. Now we must make it practical. The ordinary person, rushing helter-skelter through modern life, needs down-to-earth guidelines. In figuring out how to behave—when driving, let's say, or buying or selling or dealing with our sexuality—we need specific ethical wisdom to rely upon. A grand ideal is fine, but what does this ideal require in daily life? What in particular?

Here we come to the concept of law. While the Christian believes that right morals may be epitomized in a single word, *agapē,* he knows, too, the helpfulness of laws. Laws (if they are good ones) are the "wisdom of love."[4] They translate the grand ideal into a practical philosophy of life, a useful guide for the meeting of everyday problems. Laws are the working rules that satisfy the universal need for something more specific.

In the Judeo-Christian tradition, the classic code of laws is what we call the Ten Commandments. In the Bible story, the Hebrew people received these laws just after God, in His steadfast kindness, had delivered them from their bondage to foreign tyrants. In this way they learned how they could continue toward achieving their full potential as a people of God. In the Ten Commandments, God prohibited the worship of other gods, the making of "images" of God, and the misuse of God's name. He required the keeping of the Sabbath day and the honoring of parents. He forbade murder, adultery, theft, false witness, and coveting.

To this day, Christians believe that these commands of God express the "wisdom of love" with a simplicity and brevity matched nowhere else. Here are moral rules that have an authority in daily life which we must never disregard. They express, in specific terms, what love requires. Goodwill toward others *means* that you will not belittle God, the Source of all good, or belittle your neighbor through murder or theft, for example.

Of course other moral principles besides the Ten Commandments express what love requires. Keeping promises is an example. If you say you will adhere to an honorable agreement, you must stick by your word. Another example (one we'll return to in a moment) is that you should be, as Paul advised, "subject to the governing authorities" (Romans 13:1, RSV). In this world, goodwill toward others means supporting government and obeying the civil authorities. It means being on the side of order instead of chaos.

But just now we have to be very careful. For true

Christianity, while certain that laws (in the plural) are crucial, is at the same time certain that only one law has ultimate authority—the law of love. And curiously, a goodwill that is undefeatable and that takes the initiative for the sake of others may sometimes come into conflict with a particular commandment or moral principle.

Let me illustrate with the story of Dietrich Bonhoeffer, a brilliant young German theologian who was hanged in a Nazi concentration camp. As early as 1933 he predicted on the radio that Adolf Hitler would become a "misleader" of Germany. Later he took charge of a kind of underground seminary which trained pastors in an atmosphere of criticism of the Nazi movement. Still later he participated in the political resistance movement that had secret plans for the overthrow of Hitler. As a result of these activities he was finally arrested and thrown into prison.

Now, some thirty years after his death, Bonhoeffer is one of the most admired Christian heroes of the century—and, indeed, of all Christian history. The thing to see right here is that, in the name of love, he actually had to break certain moral principles. Though Paul advised subjection "to the governing authorities," Bonhoeffer disobeyed these authorities. And though the commandment forbids murder, and Jesus preached nonresistance, Bonhoeffer participated in a resistance movement that was ready to assassinate Hitler if necessary in order to save Germany and the world from his villainy.

It was not without pain that Bonhoeffer took these steps. He himself had written, in his book *The Cost of*

Discipleship, that Christian love "bids us not only to bear with evil and the evil person patiently, not only to refrain from treating him as he treats us, but actively to engage in heart-felt love towards him."[5] He had felt the full weight of the argument against the violent resistance of evil.

Yet Adolf Hitler brought together both mindless criminality *and* incredible political power—he could pour forth brutality upon the innocent with something very near to sheer abandon.

How, then, to love the whole people, including the great mass of innocent victims? In considering this question, Bonhoeffer finally decided to join the resistance. He did not want, as one of his friends said later, to "retreat into any sinless, righteous, pious refuge."[6] He wanted to live with Christ without fleeing from responsibility; so, for the sake of the victims, and in the name of Christ, he resisted the victimizer. And for this act of courage, he was arrested and finally executed one Sunday morning on the gallows in Flossenbürg.

What Bonhoeffer did, grew, of course, out of the abnormal circumstance in which he found himself. Though Christian moral principles forbade murder, disobedience of civil authorities, and violent resistance of evil, Bonhoeffer could not ignore the innocent millions suffering and dying under Hitler. Goodwill toward others required not a safe and secure piety, but a dangerous effort of rescue.

In short, only love has ultimate authority. The moral wisdom of good laws—especially, we may say, of the Ten Commandments—is a trustworthy guide for everyday life. But sometimes, perhaps only rarely for most of us, moral life becomes tangled and bafflingly complex. Laws may seem to conflict and provide no easy answer to the question of what to do. This is what happened to Bonhoeffer when the laws of nonresistance and obedience to governing authorities conflicted with his duty to work for the good of sufferers. Fortunately, he could turn to the law of love and make it the final arbiter—the head umpire, we might say—in the process of moral decision. *Agapē* asked him to take the initiative *for others* and not retreat from reality.

But let's make one thing clear too. If the resistance in Germany had successfully assassinated Hitler, it would very certainly have been a tragedy. For Hitler was faced with struggles and hopes and disappointments as important to him as ours are to us. He, too, was a person of worth and possibility. Had he been assassinated, it would have nullified, cruelly and suddenly, his potential for change, repentance, and growth. It would have pained the God who loves every one of His children, and it would have brought grief to those human beings, even if only a few, who felt affection for him.

I say this in order to emphasize just how wise good laws really are. They do, in fact, protect us from pain and tragedy, and we cannot overrule one, even in a noble cause, and expect everything to be rosy. Some pain, some evil, will result. Mark it down as an axiom.

But since we do, as a matter of harsh reality, live in a sinful world, sometimes, despite our wishes, we may have to choose between imperfect alternatives. No easy, painless course may be available. And that is when, if you are a Christian, you must do as Bonhoeffer did: go to *agapē* and struggle with the possibilities until, under

God, you decide which alternative is better. In this way you fulfill your duty in a situation of moral complexity, for as Paul said, "Love *is* the fulfilling of the law" (Romans 13:10, RSV, emphasis added).

I said before that on the subject of law we must proceed carefully. By now I hope the reason is clear. If laws are understood in a superficial way, they may actually obstruct mercy. A speed limit, to illustrate this whole matter another time, is a good thing, a part of the wisdom of love. But if you have a child with you who has all but stopped his breathing, you will break that speed limit, traffic permitting, in order to reach the hospital faster. Our axiom still holds; some evil results from breaking the law—if not an accident, at least the subtle undermining of respect for speed limits among those who see you. But here, as surely is obvious, a legalistic obedience would be even worse.

So you can see that whether your concern is for a great mass of people or for a single child, the morals of Christianity are flexible enough to help you do the best possible thing under the circumstances. Your duty, quite simply, is to live under the principle of self-giving love—even if, under abnormal conditions, you have to overrule the authority of other moral laws in order to do so. You must care for your neighbor even when your own survival may be imperiled, as Bonhoeffer's was in Nazi Germany. God in Christ has done this for humanity, and we must do it, too, if we are ever to succeed in relieving pain and building joy and restoring togetherness.

This last—the inner aim of Christian morals—weakens the charge some have made that Christianity tries to put an alien yoke on people. Christianity, in essence, is a vision of the universal dignity of mankind. According to its faith, men and women are meant to live in community with God and with each other. Though some may see the law of love as an enemy, as an alien yoke, the Christian says the true enemy is not love but the fear of love—the unwillingness to take risks for others.

A new kind of loving, the kind demonstrated at the cross, is the soul of the Christian's moral philosophy. New ventures of togetherness are fatally compromised, says the Christian faith, if the survival impulse controls our lives. By such a standard, efforts to achieve fellowship among the peoples of the earth are doomed forever. Christianity offers *agapē*, the very love of God Himself, saying that it alone can lift men and women out of the human jungle into a new community of brothers and sisters who care about each other.

---

[1] Langdon Gilkey, *Maker of Heaven and Earth* (New York: Doubleday & Company, Inc., 1965), p. 227.

[2] Søren Kierkegaard, *Works of Love* (New York: Harper & Row, Publishers, 1962), p. 70.

[3] William Barclay, *Ethics in a Permissive Society* (New York: Harper & Row, Publishers, 1971), p. 40.

[4] Paul Tillich, *Systematic Theology* (Chicago: University of Chicago Press, 1963), Vol. III, p. 160.

[5] Dietrich Bonhoeffer, *The Cost of Discipleship* (New York: The Macmillan Company, 1951), p. 128.

[6] Eberhard Bethge, quoted in the introduction to Dietrich Bonhoeffer, *Life Together* (New York: Harper & Row, Publishers, 1954), p. 11.

Chapter 7

The Holy Spirit: *God's Presence in the Here and Now, Part I*

After hopscotch the sirens.

I remember it well. I was five or maybe six, and we lived just off Harrison Boulevard in Boise, Idaho, in an old frame house with a porch. The kids in the neighborhood—mainly girls, most a little older than I—used to play hopscotch in the evenings. It was merry and carefree—kid stuff in the best and happiest sense.

About the time of sundown, however, my mother would call me in, supervise my bath, and gently order me into bed. Of the time I spent in bed after hopscotch, I have only one clear memory, that of the sirens—one or more a night, I think, moaning down Harrison Boulevard toward the sick or even, I used to imagine, the dead.

All of which is my earliest recollection of man's existential condition. Our existence on earth, as the philosophers are right in telling us, has its good side and its bad side. It has warmth and hostility. It has joy and sorrow. Life, in short, is double-sided, a mix of hopscotch and sirens.

For the snakes, roaches, and baboons, this state of things is hardly worth fussing over. But as I pointed out in chapter three, we who are human beings are different. We are not so bound to the environment, so much the victims of circumstance, that we cannot imagine something better. Unlike cows, we are not contented. When the good and the bad clash unharmoniously around us, we sense the discord and long for its resolution. Not happy with unrest and uncompleted lives, we seek some sort of completion, some sort of unmistakable fulfillment.

There is a simple way to put this predicament: We want something we don't have. And this is where we come, perhaps surprisingly, to the Christian doctrine of the Holy Spirit. For Christians believe that the Holy Spirit is the answer to the double-sidedness of life. The Holy Spirit enables men and women to live well even in the midst of discord.

I said this may be a surprise. The usual stereotype about getting the Spirit is at first confusing. Media treatment of various revivals and Pentecostal movements causes us to associate baptism of the Spirit with some sort of emotional binge or with an outbreak of speaking in tongues or even rolling in the aisles. It is easy to conclude that the Holy Spirit has little if anything to do with our lives in the real world. But the truth, despite all this, is that the Holy Spirit has much to do with everyday life and everyday problems. When Paul said, "Be filled with the Spirit" (Ephesians 5:18), he was not suggesting something ecstatic or pietistic. He was talking about the answer to the very real trials and dilemmas of life.

According to the Gospel of John, in a farewell statement made just before His arrest Jesus said to His disciples, " 'I will not leave you desolate; I will come to you. Yet a little while, and the world will see me no more, but you will see me' " (John 14:18, 19). He would soon leave them, and yet, paradoxically, He would not be gone. Though invisible to the eyes of the world, He would remain with them. The Father, He said, would send the Holy Spirit "in my name," and the Spirit would teach them all things and bring to their remembrance what He had said (John 14:26).

The meaning of these words, simply put, is that the experience of the Holy Spirit is the presence of Christ, the presence of God Himself. The One who walked the earth with His disciples is still here, just as He promised He would be. If the Holy Spirit is here, Jesus is present, touching lives in the here and now and helping people live above the double-sidedness of life, the mix of good and bad, of hopscotch and sirens.

In a conversation with Nicodemus, Jesus explained the advantage of having the Spirit. " 'That which is born of the flesh is flesh,' " He said, " 'and that which is born of the Spirit is spirit' " (John 3:6). Jesus meant that without the Spirit you are weak and you cannot experience fulfillment. But if you are born of the Spirit—if the Spirit grasps hold of your life—the power of the divine is at work inside you.

It may be asked at this point what the power of the divine does. Christians have said it does three things, each of which enables people to live above the double-sidedness of life.

First, the Holy Spirit produces faith. When in a famous conversation at Caesarea Philippi Peter confessed that Jesus was the Christ, his faith was not something hatched up under his own power. Jesus told him, " 'Flesh and blood has not revealed this to you, but my Father who is in heaven' " (Matthew 16:17). It was the impact of God Himself—the presence, we would say today, of the Holy Spirit—that made a believer out of Peter.

Here you can see clearly how the Holy Spirit answers a real problem of human existence. In our time, the double-sidedness of life is so confusing and discouraging that uncertainty overwhelms many people. Jack Kerouac, the beatnik novelist of the fifties, wondered whether there was anything to anticipate but the "forlorn rags of growing old." In Samuel Beckett's drama *Waiting for Godot,* Godot, who symbolizes our craving for fulfillment, is supposed to come "tomorrow" to "save us." But he never comes. That which can bring meaning and significance to life is perpetually postponed.

The Holy Spirit, however, conquers the double-sidedness of life in our age of despair by producing faith, a living and unshakable trust in the basic decency and friendliness of the universe. The Spirit produces confidence that Jesus the Messiah is a picture of the way things are. His forgiveness means that the One who put us here is merciful and kind. His power to heal means that wholeness and renewal are stronger than misery and decay. His triumph over the grave means that the entire universe is moving toward the victory of life and hope over death and despair. Human existence, therefore, is positive and beautiful. Apathy and joylessness are overcome. We can be, as Martin Luther said, "joyful, high-spirited, and eager in our relations with God and with all mankind."[1]

Second, the Holy Spirit produces love. Paul, in 1 Corinthians 13, says this is His greatest gift, perhaps for the reason that lack of love is the greatest misery. In his famous play *No Exit* Jean-Paul Sartre describes the experience of three persons who have just died and been escorted into "hell." Though surprised to find themselves in a nicely furnished room—they expected hot fires and instruments of torture—it is not long until they understand. Bickering and jealousy break out, and soon all three are miserable in one another's company. "There's no need for redhot pokers," says one character finally. "Hell is—other people."

Because of God's presence in the here and now, people can be transformed from agents of hell into agents of happiness. Through His presence among us, God creates love. He reunites the separated. He produces a drive toward togetherness, toward humanity and justice and brotherhood.

Finally, as the experience of the first disciples shows, the Holy Spirit produces the church. His presence makes a new community, a "household of faith," as the Bible puts it (Galatians 6:10). Persons of different races, backgrounds, ages, careers, and traditions come together for shared worship and shared meals and a shared commitment to the spread of faith and love in the world. What Paul calls the "fellowship of the Holy Spirit" (2 Corinthians 13:

14) saves these persons from loneliness, guilt, and fear. It also binds them together for service. Under the Spirit's impact, they spread Good News by telling about the love that Jesus Christ released into our world. They protest against apathy and injustice by calling people back to the worship of the true God. They overcome discord by personally working to bring peace and togetherness on earth. And although their witness is imperfect, a mere fragment of what it should be, their life as a church is still a tangible anticipation of what God will achieve in His creation. The church is still both a sign and an agency of hope, created by the Spirit for a world desperately needing hope.

All of this is why the doctrine of the Holy Spirit is not about pietism or overexcitement. The Spirit is the answer to actual, everyday problems. But now, having seen this, another question presents itself: How can *I* experience God's presence? How can *I* be touched by the Holy Spirit?

We have come to one of the hard questions of the Christian faith. I know of no easy answer, nor of any that could be called complete. Try as we will, this question will always leave us with a sense of mystery and paradox. Even so, some things can be said.

The first is that God's presence is not something *we* produce but something *He* gives to us. I cannot say to you or anyone else, "Do this particular thing, or adopt that particular attitude, and—presto!—God will move into your life." That would contradict a basic theme of Scripture, namely, that it is *God's act*, not our own, by which He comes into our lives.

But neither can I say, "You may want God's presence in your life, but you have nothing at all to do with whether you get it." That would also contradict a theme of Scripture, namely, that we must open the door, so to speak, to God.

The Bible expresses the whole paradox this way: " ' "Behold, I stand at the door and knock; if any one hears my voice and opens the door, I will come in to him and eat with him, and he with me" ' " (Revelation 3:20). It pictures a God whom we would never grasp hold of under our own power. He comes to the door, for we could never find Him unless He came to us. Yet when He does come to us, we can resist Him. We can refuse to open the door.

So there is no neat formula to explain how you go about experiencing God's presence in your life. For the skeptic who asks with a sneer how he can get the Spirit, there is no satisfying answer. But when a person asks the same question with a deep inner-personal seriousness, that means the Spirit has *already* begun to work. This person is already aware of his need of help from God. He has already felt a shattering of self-centeredness. The experience of rebirth, of being grasped by the Spirit of God, has already begun.

How this experience continues and develops over the long run is, once again, hard to put into words. It would be convenient to have a precise chronological account, but none is available. You cannot break down the experience of the Spirit into so many clearly definable steps. Your first step, if you tried, would be as familiar to the apostle Paul (were he with us) as to the newest Christian in town. This is because the experience of the Spirit is a continuous whole. It can be analyzed into parts, and each of these described, as the church's thinkers and teachers have done from the start. But you can never say you are completely done with one part of the experience and have moved on to something more advanced. Each of the parts is with you always.

Here is what I mean. The shattering of self-centeredness to which I just referred forms one part of the experience we are talking about and is traditionally called *repentance*. When the Holy Spirit takes over a life, He brings about a silent, inner concern over the pride, cussedness, and greed of the heart. And though it would be nice, as Kierkegaard said, to "drink down all the bitterness of sorrow in a single draught and then hurry on,"[2] it does not work this way. Repentance is a state, not a one-time heart throb. The Spirit works continually to free the individual from being "too much his own god"[3] and to help him feel a need for the true God.

Another part of the Christian's experience of the Spirit is called *conversion*. Seneca, the Roman Stoic and moralist, pronounced a harsh verdict on the human race: " 'Wicked we are, wicked we have been, and, I regret to add, wicked we always will be.' "[4] But through the Spirit's impact, the Christian knows that no person need stay the way he is. God's presence can effect a complete change of mind and attitude. The direction of life can be completely reversed—"from injustice toward justice, from inhumanity to humanity, from idols to God."[5] And yet conversion, like repentance, is not something that happens all at once. It is not the end of the road but the beginning, and along the way there are setbacks that call again and again for a change of direction.

This takes us straight to another part of the experience of the Spirit, a very beautiful part. It is that of acceptance by God. The Bible attributes it to His grace and calls it "justification by faith." These terms may seem obscure to modern ears, but they express a message of encouragement to anyone who struggles with feelings of failure and remorse. When the Spirit touches our lives, He brings assurance that *God accepts us even though we are unacceptable.* The very Maker of all things responds to our faults, even our most intimate and secret ones, with a word of forgiveness. And so we need not go around with faint heart asking, "Does God really accept me? How can I be sure He isn't rejecting me?" The Good News is really good news and not halfhearted propaganda. God, who is the most important Reality in all the universe, remains our Friend through thick and thin. He releases us from fear and assures us that we are somebody despite our failures. He frees us from self-contempt so that we may achieve our full potential as human beings.

The enormous comfort brought by the Spirit is suggested in a comment Martin Luther once made at the dinner table. " 'Mother love,' " he told his students, family, and friends, " 'is stronger than the filth and scabbiness on a child, and so the love of God toward us is stronger than the dirt that clings to us.' "[6]

But now we have come abruptly to a paradox. The

Christian experiences God's presence as a power that changes lives. But he also experiences God's presence as a willingness to show mercy, to accept those who do not deserve to be accepted. Does God cure us of evil, or does He just forgive us of it when it happens?

---

[1]John Dillenberger, ed., *Martin Luther: Selections From His Writings* (Chicago: Quadrangle Books, Inc., 1961), p. 24.

[2]Soren Kierkegaard, *Purity of Heart Is to Will One Thing* (New York: Harper & Row, Publishers, 1956), p. 44.

[3]Reinhold Niebuhr, *The Nature and Destiny of Man* (New York: Charles Scribner's Sons, 1964), Vol. II, p. 100.

[4]Quoted in William Barclay, *Turning to God* (Philadelphia: The Westminster Press, 1952), p. 12.

[5]Paul Tillich, *Systematic Theology* (Chicago: The University of Chicago Press, 1963), Vol. III, p. 219. I am heavily indebted to this work in the present chapter.

[6]*Luther's Works* (Philadelphia: Fortress Press, 1967), Vol. 54, p. 70.

Chapter 8

The Holy Spirit:
God's Presence in the Here and Now, Part II

In Christian circles you will find some persons who insist on an extremely dangerous idea. "If you rely completely on the power of the Holy Spirit," they maintain, "you can overcome sin in your life."

The idea is that God's presence in the here and now can completely transform the willing man or woman. Some have even thought that God's presence now can completely transform society. Although the persons who say these things will admit that we are deeply tainted with evil, they emphasize the power of the Spirit so strongly that theological perfectionism results. This is the view that we (or even whole societies) will be "perfect" morally, or very nearly so, if we are truly receptive to the Holy Spirit.

One of the great debates of the eighteenth century dealt with this very question. On one side was Count Zinzendorf, a German who belonged to a group of Christians called Pietists, who were fed up with orthodox Lutheranism. On the other side was the Englishman John Wesley, who founded Methodism.

In his journal Wesley recorded an exchange between himself and his German opponent. Said Zinzendorf, " 'I acknowledge no inherent perfection in this life. This is the error of errors.' "

Wesley replied, " 'But I believe that the spirit of Christ works this perfection in true Christians.' "

Zinzendorf continued, " 'By no means; all our perfection is in Christ. . . . In ourselves we are never perfect.' "[1]

At the end of the last chapter I asked, Does God cure us of evil, or does He just forgive us of it when it happens? The debate between Wesley and Zinzendorf is part of the whole effort by Christians to answer these questions. And it is not, as you might suppose, unessential religious chitchat. Everything we might say on the subject is potentially dangerous, for our understanding here has an enormous effect on our actual lives. We will see why in the next few pages.

Paul wrote, "But now that you have been set free from sin and have become slaves of God, the return you get is sanctification [that is, a holy life]" (Romans 6:22). Said John, speaking of Christ, "No one who abides in him sins; no one who sins has either seen him or known him" (1 John 3:6).

These Bible verses strongly support Wesley and the persons I mentioned at the beginning of the chapter. Taken by themselves, these Scriptural passages obviously confirm the view that we may overcome sin completely if we accept God's presence into our lives.

But these same Biblical authors also seem to support Zinzendorf. Paul admitted that sin still troubled him. "Not that I . . . am already perfect" (Philippians 3:12), he told the Philippians. And John, in the very letter I quoted from before, wrote: "If we say we have no sin, we deceive ourselves, and the truth is not in us" (1 John 1:8).

There in four brief texts you have the paradox: The Spirit, God's presence in the here and now, makes bad people into good people; yet pride, cussedness, and greed remain. Wesley argued that the Spirit works "perfection in true Christians." Zinzendorf said, No. "In ourselves we are never perfect." Strangely enough, in their own way both men were right.

John Wesley was troubled by those who held that the gospel, when it asserts that the unacceptable are accepted, frees the believer from taking seriously God's commands. He rightly maintained that the gospel both requires and makes possible obedience to these commands. Zinzendorf, on the other hand, was troubled by Wesley's tendency to imagine that God's moral demands can be completely realized. He believed that sin is never completely conquered in the life of any human being.

Where, then, lies the truth? It lies between the two extremes. The Holy Spirit grasps human lives, creating faith and love. Yet the reality of sin is never completely gone.

On the positive side, when God's presence affects someone, there is a genuine newness of life—a rejection of idols, a turning to God. More than that, the Spirit sets forth on a continuous operation of changing (or "sanctifying") that person's life. The

Spirit increases the Christian's ability to perceive evil in himself and in society, enlarges his faith in God, and strengthens his capacity to love others and to work for a better world.

Yet the believer receives, as pointed out by Paul, the "first fruits of the Spirit" (Romans 8:23), not the complete harvest. The Spirit makes unmistakable changes, and yet in this world the changes are never finished.

Right now you can see why I called the statement "You can overcome sin in your life" a dangerous idea. For in one way—let me emphasize this!—it is *very true*. With John Wesley we may say that the Spirit does bring marvelous—one can say, miraculous—improvements in the religious and ethical life of men and women. But to some the statement may suggest that moral perfection, or something very near to it, actually does occur in this life—as though in some cases God's forgiving mercy can become, for all practical purposes, irrelevant. And here is a distortion of the Scriptures that should by no means go undisputed. We are treated as though perfect by a God who sticks by us instead of rejecting us in disgust. But, as Zinzendorf said, we are never perfect in ourselves.

It may seem strange to fuss over something so seemingly theoretical and remote, but it has serious implications, not only for our personal lives but for our social existence as well. What happens, for example, to morals and justice if people become cocksure that they have attained a complete spiritual experience? The result is not that these people are free from sin (as they might imagine) but that they are blind to it.

Consider this episode from the social and political history of America. In 1830 the United States Congress passed legislation known by the remarkable name "Indian Removal Bill." By 1846 it was becoming clear that under some circumstances "removal" could include actual extermination. Surprisingly, except for a few dissenters, the great silent majority of Americans went along with this wonderfully inhuman bill. From their spiritual heritage they had acquired an exaggerated sense of having God's Spirit with them and of being God's chosen people. They were so convinced of their own righteousness that they could not see their sin. One senator rationalized what was happening by saying that only white people "used the land 'according to the intentions of the Creator.' "[2]

This shows the personal and social relevance of our subject. When a person or society overestimates the impact of God's presence and forgets the reality of sin, the effect is deadly. Evil increases, and those involved remain blissfully ignorant of what they are doing.

But if the dangerous idea I mentioned as the chapter began is potentially misleading, it is also, in its own way, very true. The Christian heritage includes a deep confidence that God's presence in the here and now can create better persons and a better world. We may see how important this is by asking what would happen if the Holy Spirit were to disappear. Suppose that you or your society dwelt so much on the reality of sin that you began to forget God's power. How would this affect morality and justice?

Here Martin Luther can help us, though in a dubious

way. This brilliant and sensitive man knew very well the reality of sin, but he underestimated the Holy Spirit's power to correct social injustices. And this led to his refusal to take God's commandments seriously where human society was concerned. "An earthly kingdom cannot exist without inequality of persons," he wrote pessimistically. "Some must be free, others serfs."[3]

You can imagine how a similar moral defeatism might have affected the black race in America during the past twenty years. Had Martin Luther King, like the one for whom he was named, considered God's Spirit too weak and flabby to change the institutions of society, black people might still be riding in the back of the buses.

So again you can see that the doctrine of the Spirit has immediate personal and social relevance. If we underestimate God's presence, the result is defeatism. The spectacle of evil goes unmolested, and there can be no significant strides toward human dignity and fellowship.

Now I am going to repeat what I have said in the chapter so far—but from a different angle. It is time to acknowledge an assumption that runs through this book—and through any book written with conviction. This is the assumption that human beings can acquire genuine knowledge. We can actually distinguish what is true from what is false. You can see how important this assumption is when you consider what would happen if no one accepted it. Men and women, quite simply, would cease to have anything important to talk about.

But most persons do have something important to talk about—or act as though they do. And the

Christian attributes this to God's Spirit at work in the here and now. If we can know the truth at all, it is because God has given it to us. But how much has He given to us? Do we know the whole truth, or must we trust God to forgive our intellectual mistakes?

The reader of the first part of the chapter will not be surprised when I say that the Spirit both guides us into truth and forgives us when we misunderstand. Here, as in the area of moral life, the believer receives the "first fruits" of the Spirit, not the complete harvest.

Even so, many persons (outside Christendom as well as inside) veer toward being cocksure about their own knowledge. They never ask for forgiveness of their theological errors.

For such persons Ellen White has written, "We have many lessons to learn, and many, many to unlearn. God and heaven alone are infallible."[4] But such humility is hard to find. Within Protestantism, theological conceit has run so rampant that Paul Tillich declared, "[The Protestant church's] *greatest downfall* has been its claim that it has, by virtue of 'pure doctrine,' become the invulnerable possessor of the truth. It has not understood that to stand [in a situation of sin] . . . means to stand not only in unrighteousness but also in error."[5]

Some people are surprised to learn that even the heroes of Scripture wrote with humility. Paul was an inspired man convinced that God had given him a knowledge of the truth. Yet when he discussed the gifts of the Spirit in 1 Corinthians 13:9, he stated that "our knowledge is imperfect and our prophecy is imperfect."

This is enormously important to think about. People who exaggerate their experience with the Spirit—who, unlike Paul, claim to have the whole truth—are susceptible to two tragic distortions of religious faith. One is spiritual arrogance, the kind of conceit and self-satisfaction that blinds people to new truth. History gives an example in the preachers who during slavery went about defending it in the name of Christian religion.

The other distortion is intolerance. Intolerance grew in the Roman Church, as everyone knows, issuing in outrageous persecutions. It developed in Protestants as well. Martin Luther urged the use of the sword against the Anabaptist sect. John Calvin presided over the death of Michael Servetus, who was burned at the stake for heresy.

The lesson here is that all claims to ultimacy in the knowledge of truth are, on the face of it, corrupt. *All knowledge and all prophecy are imperfect,* and it is not too much to say that the person who denies this is a dangerous menace in God's creation. Had Paul himself not admitted it, we might still be stuck with his toleration of the institution of slavery. Fortunately for many, God in His wisdom helped Christendom finally recognize that the truth on this matter went beyond even the knowledge of the great apostle Paul.

Yet here, as in the realm of justice and morals, it is disastrous to underestimate the Spirit's power. In the extreme (as when people lose faith in God and attribute everything to chance) this leads to the view that truth is an illusion. It produces skepticism and doubt so corrosive that life becomes futile and unrewarding. If you cannot know what your existence is about, what is the use in taking it seriously?

This is why in periods of deep skepticism men and women reach out desperately for some kind of salvation. Stricken with doubt, they cry out for some revelation, some truth to give them comfort. Reinhold Niebuhr points to Germany in the pre-Nazi period as an example of how dangerous to civilization this can be.[6] The cultural leadership was then afflicted with serious doubt about the possibility of finding genuine truth. The country was therefore vulnerable to promises of salvation and comfort, which helps explain why the fanatical political ideology of Adolf Hitler could grip many of Germany's best people. Perplexed with uncertainty, and therefore by a sense of meaninglessness, these people leaped with sudden blindness to the new religion, the new sense of certainty and assurance, that Hitler offered.

Once more you can see that the way the Spirit is understood affects the lives of real people in the real world. Where it is believed that God is really present, people can be confident that the truth is knowable. They are saved from uncertainty and meaninglessness and are not half so susceptible to sudden, false religions such as that of Hitler. At the same time a refusal to overestimate the presence of the Spirit helps people to avoid blindness and intolerance. It leads to a recognition that our truth is imperfect and that there are always new truths to learn and new errors to reject.

I said near the beginning of the last chapter that we, unlike the cows, are not contented. Not happy with our unrest and uncompleted lives, we seek some sort of unmistakable fulfillment. According to the Christian faith, the Holy Spirit provides that unmistakable fulfillment. God's presence breaks into human lives, giving faith so there is not despair, love so there is not indifference, the church so people may band together in hope and work together for peace.

Yet the fulfillment God provides, though clear and unmistakable, is not complete. God's presence in the here and now is experienced only as "first fruits." As I have tried to show, understanding what this means has everything to do with our everyday affairs and with the justice of our actual societies.

Now I have a final point to make. God's presence, as Paul affirms, is "the guarantee of our inheritance" (Ephesians 1:14). By providing unmistakable (though incomplete) fulfillment now, the Spirit shows the Christian that his hope for a completed life is not a flimsy hope. It is not a hope based, as skeptics say, on pleasant but improbable stories from the past. It is based on the indisputable fact that I and others are experiencing God's presence now.

This certainty is why, in a world of hopscotch and sirens, the Christian can cope. The ambulance—moaning down the boulevard to fetch the sick and even the dead—does not have the last word in the universe. God does.

---

[1]Quoted in Reinhold Niebuhr, *The Nature and Destiny of Man* (New York: Charles Scribner's Sons, 1964), Vol. II, p. 174. I am greatly indebted to this work in the present chapter.

[2]Martin E. Marty, *Righteous Empire: The Protestant Experience in America* (New York: The Dial Press, 1970), p. 7.

[3] Cited in a footnote in Niebuhr, Vol. II, pp. 193, 194.

[4] Ellen White, *Selected Messages* (Washington, D.C.: Review and Herald Publishing Association, 1958), Book One, p. 37.

[5] Paul Tillich, *The Protestant Era* (Chicago: The University of Chicago Press, 1957), p. 200, italics added.

[6] See Niebuhr, Vol. II, p. 239.

Chapter 9

The Sabbath: *Day of Rest and Worship*

Who has finished his life without wondering what things were like in the beginning and how they became the way they are now? I suppose no one has. Ancient stories of beginnings attest that if we moderns pose these questions and brood upon their mystery, so did our ancestors. The people who recited and wrote down these ancient stories apparently could not live without some explanation, some understanding of how everything began.

This fascination with beginnings stems from our desire to know who, or what, is at the bottom of things. Who, or what, is responsible for our existence? The subject of this chapter has to do with this very question. It is the Sabbath, the day of rest mentioned in the Hebrew Creation story. Yet I want to do an odd thing: introduce the chapter with an episode from a very different story of beginnings, the Babylonian creation epic.[1] You will see why in a moment.

The episode begins when the children in the family

of a Babylonian god cause a great disturbance with their merrymaking, and someone advises their father to destroy them—"that by day you may find rest, that by night you may sleep."

Rest matters much to this captious old divinity, and his face grows "bright with joy" at the suggestion. But before he can murder his sons, they, having learned of his intentions, murder him. Then a struggle ensues between the gods who approve the murder and those who want to avenge it. When it is finished, a god named Marduk has triumphed over Tiamat, split her in two like a fish, and made the sky with one half of her and the earth with the other. Now even the rebels who had fought with Tiamat acknowledge that Marduk is king.

The prospering Marduk proposes a great complex of buildings, called Babylon, to house himself and those who have fought with him against Tiamat. But when the rebel gods learn that Marduk will build this Babylon, they become worried. The ancient documents are fragmentary here, but the rebel gods apparently fear they will become slaves to the great gods. Because they fear they will be saddled forever with the work of running the universe, they appeal to Marduk for assurance that this will not happen.

And here we find out how *we* got here. The gods want to avert menial and everlasting labor, and Marduk has a bright idea. He will make . . . us! He will produce, he says, a "lowly, primitive creature," and " 'man' shall be his name." A kind of puppet, this lowly creature will be charged with "service" so that "the gods may have rest."

As in many stories of beginnings from various parts of the world, a curious theme presents itself: the theme of "divine rest," the idea that the gods are always trying to achieve a state of peace and quiet for themselves. You can see that the urge for rest permeates the episode from the beginning to the end, when the Babylonian gods make our race, not for some high destiny but as a convenience to themselves. In the very act of creating us, these brawling, irascible deities push us away. They make us slaves, puppets, mere useful furniture in the universe. Fellowship and communion between us and them are no object. A population of hacks—to get the "drudgework" done—is all they want. We are their exploitable handiwork.

Other documents from the ancient Near East forbid too simple a sketch. The relationship between the people and their gods is not always so cynical as in this creation story. There is even talk in some documents of personal deities who protect individuals and intercede for them among the "high gods."

Yet the creation epic, so important because it purports to explain how things began and why they came to be the way they are, contains no comforting word about the deities. These high gods, indifferent or even hostile to man, care mainly about themselves. They want their rest, their permanent, carefree, no-risk, easy-sleeping holiday in the house of Marduk.

Strange to say, the theme of divine rest also appears in Scripture. "Thus the heavens and the earth were finished, and all the host of them," says the Book of Genesis. "And on the seventh day God finished his work which he had done, and he rested on the seventh day from all his work which he had done" (Genesis 2:1, 2).

What shall we make of this? Is the God of Abraham, Isaac, and Jacob contaminated by the low and petty ways of Marduk? Is this rest the hint of a scoundrel?

You know well enough that, this far into a book, I'm not going to throw over all I've been saying and call God a scoundrel. But why not? Here is this rest idea. Well, we have stopped too soon. The writer of the passage adds, "So God blessed the seventh day and hallowed it, because on it God rested from all his work which he had done" (Genesis 2:3; two other passages, Exodus 20:11 and Exodus 31:17, connect the "divine rest" with the Sabbath).

What these words mean will occupy us for the rest of the chapter. It is enough now to say that they have great significance. The theme of divine rest does appear in Scripture, but in a unique way. God rests for a day. He gives the world a creation Sabbath.[2] And as we will see, this Sabbath sings out a loud, joyous, unmistakable dissent. If some have believed that the gods make us to be slaves and then turn away, the Sabbath denies it—in thunder! God does not turn away from His world, says the Sabbath day. He turns toward it. He does not fling down serfdom on the beings He has made. He gives them a gift: Himself.

Yet who reflects upon this holy Sabbath? Who takes it seriously? Except for Jewish believers and a very small minority of Protestant Christians, no one does. Although many persons study the Creation story, most treat the seventh day as a theological wallflower worthy of little or no attention. Yet to neglect the Sabbath is to neglect one of the greatest of God's gifts and one of the most vivid of His symbols.

You may sense already why I am saying this. Everyone knows that pessimism about the human condition did not pass away with the fall of Babylonian civilization. As modern literature and philosophy attest, it bedevils the modern person as it did his ancient brother and sister. And if long ago the Sabbath was a song of joy, this gift of God can be a song of joy today, affirming the goodness of our existence.

The theme of God's rest may depress us in the Babylonian creation epic, but in the context of Old Testament theology, it communicates assurance and hope. It expresses some very important things. God's rest tells us, first of all, that He is free to decide what to do and when to stop. What if our Maker had been a vague, impersonal force in the universe, a self-evolving process with no will of its own and no freedom to stop? We would be the creatures of a great cosmic neuter not only uncaring but unable to care. It would be as useless to dwell upon this maker's significance for our lives as to ponder the meaning of toenail growth. Such a maker would inspire no sermons or prayers, no faith or virtue.

A God who rests, however, can chart His own activity. If He wishes, He can cease from creating and get to know the creatures and the world He has made. And that is what, according to Scripture, God did. By resting He showed a more than passing interest in us. Instead of leaving us to a sinister or meaningless fate, He stopped and made us the object of His love.

Now we can startle ourselves, as will happen if we have a sense of wonder, by saying, "God loves us . . . me! my friends! my enemies! the earth!" This thought can dazzle us and fill us with a hearty, unspeakable cheer, because on the seventh day God linked Himself "with the being and purpose and course of the world, with the history of man."[3]

Let me acknowledge a question before going on. Isn't it quite ridiculous to think of God as resting? Did God get tired? And if He did, and rested, why didn't things start falling apart?

Here is an obvious problem, but it is not so difficult as it may seem. Our language about God is a human language. It's the only one we have. Knowing this makes us admit (if we are thoughtful!) that our words about God never describe Him literally. We use human terms, but that does not make God Himself human. He is not just like us. We say, for example, that God is our Father, but we don't mean that He has a wife.

By the same logic we can say God rested without meaning that He got winded or decided to retire. By resting God declared, in effect, "I am free and sovereign, and I have decided to care, to get involved." When we speak of His rest, this is what we mean, and not that He became tired. As the Old Testament itself declares, "He does not faint or grow weary" (Isaiah 40:28).

Now we make a transition—and, I may say, a momentous one. Turning from divine rest to human rest, as we are about to do, would never have occurred to the readers of the Babylonian creation epic. In that story, rest is a luxury for the gods, not for men and women. Yet in Genesis God makes the day of His rest a day of rest for His creatures, a day set apart. He blesses and hallows the Sabbath. He shares *His* rest with *us*.

You can see what an odd thing (by our standards) this is. God gives His creatures a holiday before they have had any workdays—a day of rest before they have done anything to exhaust themselves. It is a strange sequence (what employer would adopt it?) and a telling reminder of how God loves us right from the start. There is no waiting to see how we perform, no test to determine whether it is worthwhile for God to show an interest in us. He loves us before we love Him.

And there is more—the clear inference that God made us to be very like Himself. When God "blessed the seventh day," making it the Sabbath, He gave us a living token of what He meant our destiny to be. He said, in effect, "As My rest shows that I am free, the Sabbath shows that you are free. As My rest shows that I love you, the Sabbath shows (or can show) that you love Me."

Let's consider the first point. A person so tethered to his work that he can never leave it, never rest from it, utterly lacks control over his life. He is a slave. But the Sabbath shows that God did not invent slaves to do His important business. Although He gave us a work—to make the earth an ordered, livable place (see Genesis 1:26-28)—He also gave us release from our work. He gave us an exodus from labor, a capacity to stop what we are doing, which implies the ability to determine our own activity. In a word, He made us free.

As God in His freedom decides to love us, we in our

freedom may decide to love God. This is the second meaning of human rest. If we set aside our daily toil on the Sabbath day, we acknowledge that beyond our efforts to make the world an ordered, livable place is the One who gave us the will to try. We admit that beyond our machine shops and laboratories is the One who made us. He is our strength and sure foundation.

The answer to human problems is not, as some may suppose, to flee away from things, to renounce technical civilization for a vague spiritual experience. Nor is it the answer to ignore the Eternal and bow down before things—as if jetports and computers could make us whole. The answer, as Abraham Heschel declares, is to work with things, according to God's command, but to be in love with eternity. "Things are our tools," but God is our mate.[4]

The Sabbath offers us an opportunity to say this. If we rest, it is not only a deliverance from "clattering commerce"[5] but also a form of worship. By singing, praying, and listening on the Sabbath, by enjoying peaceful leisure and close friendship with one another, we not only sense God's presence but affirm that He is indeed the final joy of all created things.

It is here that we can see the relation of the Sabbath to the other days, for if the Sabbath turns us to God, it prepares us for our work. "The Sabbath is the inspirer," writes Heschel, "the other days the inspired."[6] Rest and worship renew our faith and bring blessedness, joy, and peace. We receive a heightened sense of life and of what our existence is truly about. And it carries through the days of work that follow.

Now, I believe that the Sabbath experience has a continuing validity. Jesus told us, " 'The sabbath was made for man' " (Mark 2:27), and that seems to me as true today as when He uttered it. Yet not many Christians would agree. What would I say if I were asked to explain myself?

I would make two basic points: the Sabbath is a sign of meaning and it is a form of discipline. Then I would say, with Albert Camus and many others, that in our time "the meaning of life is the most urgent of questions."[7] I would go on to say with the daily newspapers that through violence, apathy, and double-dealing, men and women every day flout moral values as if there were no higher authority in the universe than themselves. Finally I would ask whether the Sabbath experience—of assurance and commitment to higher authority—isn't, after all, what we need.

According to the prophet, God told the Israelites to " 'hallow my sabbaths that they may be a sign between me and you, that you may know that I the Lord am your God' " (Ezekiel 20:20). Through the Sabbath, God intended that His people would apprehend a meaning beyond what meets the eye. He intended that on His day of rest they would experience in a special way the "Love that moves the sun and all the stars."

Without such an experience, life turns very bleak. What meets the eye—mere facts, mere observable data—can stifle and even terrify us. Mircea Eliade asks how man can "tolerate the catastrophes and horrors of history—from collective deportations and massacres to atomic bombings—if beyond them he can glimpse no sign, no transhistorical meaning."[8] How, indeed? If there is no Reality Beyond, what is to keep us from terror? What is to save us from despair?

The Sabbath is a sign of Reality Beyond, a sign, as Ellen White has said, "of creative and redeeming power."[9] An end to labor on the seventh day will not magically create faith in the heart of the unbeliever. But for those who acknowledge God, the Sabbath brings a vivid experience of His presence and steadfast love. It is God's day to be with us in a special fellowship, to reassure us against doubt and discouragement, to defend us against terror, and to remind us of the beauty and promise in our existence. "The Sabbath," Abraham Heschel tells us, "comes like a caress, wiping away fear, sorrow and somber memories."[10]

But if the Sabbath is a sign of meaning, it is also a defense against the fickleness of the human heart. We easily forget our true Lord and easily exalt some thing, idea, or ambition above our Maker—and suffer as a consequence. God made the Sabbath a law (not only a gift) in order to protect us against this fickleness. (See Exodus 20:8-11, where the law of the Sabbath is set down. In Exodus 16:29 the Sabbath is perceived as a gift.)

So here is the other reason for the Sabbath: it is a discipline that keeps us in touch with our Maker despite the clamor of lesser gods. The law of Sabbath-keeping gives us—every week—a time for stillness and peace, a time to orient our lives toward the True Center of existence. It frees us from bondage to the ordinary and lets us see, despite ourselves, the One who gave us our being and asks our obedience.

Who, or what, is at the bottom of things? Each week the Sabbath signals the answer: a God of love and mercy gave us our existence. As a gift, the Sabbath reassures us. As a law, it disciplines our fickle hearts. And for those who keep the Sabbath by stopping from their labor to rest and worship, the coming of its holy hours is like an announcement of joy.

It is as though God says, "Welcome to a holiday of hope."

---

[1]The version of the Babylonian creation epic quoted here appears in *Documents From Old Testament Times,* edited by D. Winton Thomas (New York: Harper & Row, Publishers, 1961), pp. 3-16.

[2]Niels-Erik Andreasen has written on the creation Sabbath in *The Old Testament Sabbath* (Missoula, Montana: The Society of Biblical Literature, 1972), pages 174-199. I am indebted to Andreasen's work in my remarks on "divine rest" in the Babylonian creation epic, and in my attempt to relate this rest to that in the Biblical account.

[3]Karl Barth, *Church Dogmatics,* III, Part 1 (Edinburgh: T. & T. Clark, 1958), p. 216.

[4]See *The Sabbath: Its Meaning for Modern Man,* by Abraham Joshua Heschel (New York: Harper & Row, Publishers, 1966), p. 48.

[5]*Ibid.,* p. 13.

[6]*Ibid.,* p. 22.

[7]Albert Camus, *The Myth of Sisyphus* (New York: Vintage Books, 1955), p. 4.

[8]*Cosmos and History: The Myth of the Eternal Return* (New York: Harper & Row, Publishers, 1954), p. 151.

[9]Ellen G. White, *Education* (Mountain View, California: Pacific Press Publishing Association, 1952), p. 250.

[10]*The Sabbath: Its Meaning for Modern Man,* p. 68.

Chapter 10

The Human Story:
Hope, Purpose, and Everyday Life

You do not have to look long or very hard at government, labor, education, the military, the church, or any other institution before you have plenty of reason to want to change things. It is the same when you consider the oppression of minorities, the suffering of the hungry, the fear of those who can't walk their streets in safety. If you have heart and if you have eyes, you never lack reason to hope for something better.

But suppose that just when you are dreaming your best dreams and hoping your best hopes, a philosopher comes along and calls you foolish. Suppose he announces his views in a single, pungent sentence: "Everything is always the same." It would cause grave discouragement.

Here is why. If his words were true, you would have to discard your hopes. For if everything were always the same, there would be no use in trying anything, no use in running after any goals or seeking any changes. Under conditions of everlasting sameness, nothing you could do would help.

I remember a friend who returned from army basic training with a hundred stories about the way drill sergeants had made life miserable for eight weeks. It wasn't long after training began, he said, until a standard cynical statement came into vogue in the barracks as a reply to questions. The statement was: "It doesn't matter." Whether you were asked if your feet were blistered, or if you thought the food would be better tomorrow, or if you could tolerate the hollering another day, "It doesn't matter" was the answer. It was a joke of sorts, but more than that. In basic training there was no way out, no possibility of change. You were trapped. You could not escape the sneering drill sergeants, and so nothing mattered anymore. There was nothing you could do anyway.

It may surprise you, but a long time ago a famous philosopher-poet actually did say that "everything is always the same," making life itself a kind of boot camp. Lucretius, a Roman and an exponent of what we now call "classical naturalism," wrote in the first century before Christ: "All things remain the same even if you should outlast all the ages in living; and still more would you see them the same if you should never come to die."[1]

You can see that this is devastating talk. If true, the meaning of our lives on earth is cancelled out, annulled like a bad marriage into nothingness. There is nothing to achieve, no place to go, no motive to transform our world. We are all like soldiers in boot camp, so imprisoned by the forces around us that nothing really matters.

Before life on earth can have actual meaning for any

of us, we have to be able to think in terms of a goal. We have to believe in the possibility of the new, of change, of something better. We have to believe that we are moving toward some kind of clear, unmistakable fulfillment. Without these things, our existence and that of our society is without significance and purpose. And the story of the human family is an empty story, so much cold and meaningless chronology.

A big part of the Good News is that the Christian way of looking at the human story, unlike that of classical naturalism, is positive and hopeful. Instead of cold chronology, the story becomes one of purpose and meaning. It is a story in which human striving and suffering are part of a movement toward magnificent fulfillment.

This way of understanding the story theologians call the "Christian doctrine of history." That is, I know, an obscure phrase—rather like a soupy morning fog—and yet the doctrine of history has a meaning so simple it will surprise you and so beautiful you will want to shout. It is this, that there is a continuing relationship between the mud, rocks, people, and events that make up the human story and the God who made all things. Somehow the earth and humanity are touched by saving power, by divine purpose.

My friend in boot camp might have found some peace and meaning through thoughtful meditation late at night, or through the belief that there was a life beyond the joyless regimentation of boot camp. But he could not find meaning in the actual goings-on around him, in the actual story of his everyday life. For Lucretius the whole of life was like that, but for

Christianity it is different. Life is decidedly not like boot camp. There is meaning in the goings-on around us, in the actual story of our everyday life.

The one surpassing reason for this, according to the Christian faith, is that God has put Himself right into the middle of the human story. He did this first of all by creating the setting and the players in the story. And to the players He gave the power to be free and original, to make history instead of being controlled entirely by forces outside themselves. This is why we can speak of a story rather than a puppet show. The players can produce the new, the unique, the unexpected.

But God is in the middle of the human story in another way: He lifts His mighty hand and His outstretched arm (Deuteronomy 26:8) in order to assure the working out of His own high purposes. If the prophets of Israel were sure of one thing above all, it was that God Himself was touching their history, nudging it along toward the new and the better. Even on the occasion of rebellion and tragedy for Israel, as when her people were transplanted ruthlessly across a desert to Babylon, God was working through the evil situation to achieve His aims and to create new opportunity and new hope.

I don't mean that every detail of the human story develops out of divine necessity, as though God Himself decreed the exact course of events on the earth. That would contradict the freedom and spontaneity which He has given to all of us. It would reduce the human story to a series of preplanned events, and we would be not so much the makers of history as mere pawns on a chessboard.

I do mean, however, that God is ultimately in charge. His creatures are free to do good and evil, but the evil can never destroy the good nor prevent the true aim of the human story. Thus the Hebrews never felt imprisoned by circumstance. They believed in the possibility of the new. They looked ahead to the fulfillment of God's purposes. Their story never seemed cold and empty to them. They were a movement; they were going somewhere.

But now we come to an astonishing difference between the prophets of the Old Testament and the writers of the New Testament. While the prophets were always looking ahead to a decisive act of God that would really change things, the New Testament writers insisted that this decisive act had already occurred. God had revealed Himself on the earth in the person of Jesus Christ and had changed the shape of history.

Here it is good to begin with the words of Jesus Himself: " 'The time is fulfilled, and the kingdom of God is at hand' " (Mark 1:15). Again, having cast out a demon, He said, " 'But if it is by the finger of God that I cast out demons, then the kingdom of God has come upon you' " (Luke 11:20). On another occasion the Pharisees asked Him when the kingdom would come, and He replied, " 'For behold, the kingdom of God is in the midst of you' " (Luke 17:21). As these sayings indicate, *Jesus associated Himself with the arrival of God's kingdom. He attached to Himself decisive significance.*

This claim might have remained forever a mere assertion—save for one thing: the Resurrection. Having died, this Man could not be contained by death. The disciples, having buried Him, later saw Him alive, and for them that was everything. It confirmed everything He had said about Himself, and they became convinced that the supreme miracle of history had taken place. Jesus had associated Himself with the kingdom, and what He said was true. A new age really had begun.

Paul affirms, "If Christ has not been raised, your faith is futile" (1 Corinthians 15:17). If Jesus had been one more unfortunate gone to the tomb, human hopes would not have been increased by His life but lessened. He would not so much have overcome the evil powers as He would have been their most pathetic victim. But He did not stay in the tomb. Having been swallowed up by death, He then became, as Christians believe, the conqueror of death—the master even of the last great enemy itself.

What this means for the human story is breathtaking. It guarantees that the story will end well, stopping with neither a bang nor a whimper but with the fulfillment of God's purposes. When a story brims with happy occasions and characters who fulfill their lives but ends with the meaningless slaughter of everyone, it is fundamentally a tragic story. Or when a story tells of suffering and struggle but never has a real ending because the suffering and struggle go on and on and on—that story is tragic too. But if a story portrays suffering and struggle and then ends well, with the people's lives fulfilled and suffering overcome, it is fundamentally a happy, meaningful story.

Because of the Resurrection, the human story, to

put it all very simply, is a story you can feel good about. Yet Jesus said something once that, in view of this, may seem very strange. " 'If any man would come after me,' He told the disciples, 'let him . . . take up his cross and follow me' " (Matthew 16:24). According to Christian faith, the events surrounding the cross are a source of power, saving the whole story of man, making it into something beautiful and good. But that is not all. The cross is also the model for our lives.

This means, quite plainly, that although the kingdom has come and Jesus has defeated the armies of evil, we must still suffer in a world where evil has a grip. And so we have come to another paradox: Even though evil has been defeated, it is still in there pitching. Even though the kingdom *has* come, it *will* come. The good ending is still future.

This paradox has great significance for our individual and collective lives. First of all, to say that the kingdom *has* come means that Jesus Christ is already reigning. He has already, in Paul's phrase, "disarmed the principalities and powers" (Colossians 2:15). I suppose everyone knows the caricature that has all Christians waiting passively for "pie in the sky by and by." But those Christians who do so do not know true Christianity, and those skeptics who think Christians in general do so, do not know it either. God's salvation is not limited to some future, supernatural time and place. From the earliest times, believers have testified that He is at work in the here and now and that He will continue to work until "he has put all his enemies under his feet" (1 Corinthians 15:25).

In the history of Christian faith, some, despite the words of Scripture, have thought an unbridgeable gap separates God's kingdom from the earth. They have found it hard to imagine that God's justice ever touches the earth, ever alters the institutions of society. Their existence and influence account in part for the caricature I just referred to. But if we go back to the basic documents of Christianity, we will not miss the conviction that God is in charge *here* and that life *here* can be changed. Not only did the writers of Scripture say that men and women should work for justice, peace, and love, but they also said it is not hopeless to do so. They held that the human story always contains new possibilities for the good. Defeatism is never appropriate.

This avoids, as we have seen, the classical naturalism of Lucretius, which reduces the human story to everlasting sameness. It also avoids the tragic view of the Greeks, for whom the human story did not run toward eventual fulfillment, but in a circle. For them the story was one of ups and downs. When things went well, they were certain, sooner or later, to decay. It was a circle of greatness and tragedy that could not be broken, and there could be no true hope for the human story. This explains the Greeks' yearning to be free from the world. It is why, for Platonism, the "world of sight" was a "prison house."[2]

Christianity avoids, finally, the mystical view of the human story. Most highly developed in the East, as in Hinduism and Buddhism, mysticism represents, once again, a denial that the story has meaning in itself. For the mystic it is necessary to live on the earth, to act reasonably, and to be compassionate. But the human story itself does not run toward a goal, and there is no motivation to bring about real change, no impulse to enlarge the scope of human dignity and justice. The difficulties of life, according to mysticism, are unconquerable, and the only way to cope is to live above the human story while living in it. The mystic seeks to live as someone who has already returned to the Ultimate One. It is a goal not easy for us in the West to understand, yet this much is clear: The mystic does not consider everyday occurrences to have true reality, nor does he have hope that everyday life can be changed.[3]

The Christian vision, with its certainty that Jesus Christ defeated the armies of evil and inaugurated a new age, stands in contrast to all this. It says that everything is *not* always the same, that the world is *not* a prison house, that mystical escape is *not* the only way to cope. The new can take place, and we do not have to discard our hopes for a better world.

Yet alongside the optimism of the Christian faith there remains the cross, standing stark on the rim of the earth and telling all who see it that misery and pain have not yet fled away. The just and the unjust alike suffer still.

This means that the kingdom in its fullness has not yet come. Though the armies of evil have been defeated, they have not yet surrendered. We are not yet done with the crime, poverty, boredom, guilt, touchiness, slaughter, and natural disaster that plague our otherwise beautiful world. It remains in the future for God to put His splendid last touch on the human story.

Jesus Himself assured His followers that this would happen. After predicting that soon He would suffer, He further revealed that "the son of man is to come with angels in the glory of his Father" (Matthew 16:27). The early church took faith in what He said, believing that He would indeed return and that He would make "a new heaven and a new earth" (Revelation 21:1).

What does this mean? How does faith that the kingdom will come in fullness affect the human story? We will see that it has a profound effect, and that speaking of Christ's return is not, as some believe, a matter of irrelevant attentiveness to the by-and-by.

In the first place, the belief that Jesus will appear again and that "when he appears we shall be like him" (1 John 3:2) means this: Evil is not a second god with power to overthrow the good completely. Our existence on earth will never ultimately contradict the Creator's intentions. Such a realization forms the basis—in the here and now!—for a hope that does not die, for triumph over sullenness and pessimism.

Yet the Christian hope differs from other kinds of hope, and the distinction must be clearly seen. One of these other kinds is evolutionary optimism, which holds that the human story is a matter of infinite progress toward perfection. Another is utopianism, the dream of revolutionaries, which anticipates a stage in the human story when evil will be completely conquered.

The events of the twentieth century have weakened —some would say have demolished—both these hopes.

War, the crises of environment, the persistence of loneliness in crowded, wealthy societies have all stabbed optimism in the back, just as the elaborate cruelties done in Marx' name have cast grave doubt upon the vision of utopianism. For Christianity, however, these events are neither a surprise, nor an excuse to quit trying, nor a cause for despair.

Why are they not a surprise? Christianity recognizes the tenacity of evil and takes it more seriously than these alternative forms of hope. Through its belief in the Second Coming, Christianity provides a vantage point from which to criticize naive optimism. The Christian knows that life in the here and now is a continual struggle against evil and that while there are victories, they are never complete. People who are free to do good are free to do evil also. When the power of good increases (as when, for example, people become sensitive to economic inequalities), the power of evil can increase as well (as when tyranny becomes the means to deal with these inequalities).

But why is the persistence of evil not an excuse to quit trying? Again, the Christian's faith that the kingdom *will* come decides the answer. In the end, God Himself will judge and make right the evil of the world. That which is destructive will be exposed and separated out so that the harmony of the universe may be restored.

Christians call this the last judgment, and if taken seriously, it greatly affects life in the here and now. In the first place, the judgment implies that we have the power to distinguish between good and evil. Someone may be tempted in a world of labyrinthine complexity to throw up his hands and say there is no use trying to know what is right. Today's moral riddles are beyond comprehension. But that attitude will not do. Even if evil masquerades as a positive good (as when women are held down in the name of motherhood or when pornography is praised as a liberating force), it can be exposed for what it really is. And it must be. In the second place, the last judgment means that whether we live on the side of good or evil has eternal consequences. God's creatures can conceivably miss His destination for them.

We may ask, finally, why the persistence of evil need not cause despair. And again we come to the Christian's faith that God will put a splendid last touch on the human story. The doctrine of the resurrection of the body—another great theme of the church's theology—expresses the Christian's hope and confidence. I do not propose to explain how God could accomplish something as fantastic as the resurrection of dead bodies. But what He will do has a meaning that can be stated clearly, and that, after all, is what matters.

The resurrection of the body is first of all a resounding No to views that deny the meaningfulness of the human story. The Biblical account affirms the goodness of Creation from the perspective of the past: In the beginning God saw everything He had made and called it "very good." The resurrection affirms the goodness of Creation from the perspective of the future: In the end God does not dismantle our present mode of life but affirms it. Instead of changing those He saves into, say, formless spirits, He resurrects their bodies.

If God did otherwise, it would signify His distaste for the body, but He is not in the least sorry that He gave us bodies and put us in a world of dirt, rocks, and growing things. He is overjoyed that we can have sex, taste apples, plant gardens, construct buildings, and go to the beach. God is only sorry about sin—the self-love that disrupts the harmony of creation—and it is that, not the glory of the body, that He intends to devastate.

All that I've said in this chapter boils down in the end to four brief, unsensational words: The human story matters. God will preserve, not destroy, the significance of our individual and collective lives. We can see, smell, hear, touch, and taste. We can think and create and love. And our mode of being has eternal worth.

So if the four words are unsensational, the idea they express is not. That the human story matters is a bit of good news that makes the sports page seem by comparison as exciting as a catalog of zip codes. This, indeed, is the Good News without which no other good news is even possible. It is the Good News without which the birth of a baby would bring infinite boredom. But the birth of a baby is far more than boredom. It is a joy wrapped up in jubilation. When you have the Good News—inside of you as part of your deepest self—it does everything for births, and everything for lives and whole communities and even the world itself.

I said before that it is the Spirit, God's presence in the here and now, that puts the Good News into your heart and bones. When He does, and you believe with all your soul and might that the human story matters, you will go out tomorrow—today!—to wrestle the demons. And I won't bother to say, "Good luck!" Luck is not the name of the game in the kingdom of God. The demons have had it.

---

[1]Quoted in Reinhold Niebuhr, *The Nature and Destiny of Man* (New York: Charles Scribner's Sons, 1964), Vol. II, p. 9.

[2]Plato, *The Republic*, 517.

[3]I am indebted in these paragraphs to Paul Tillich's discussion on pages 350-352 of *Systematic Theology* (Chicago: The University of Chicago Press, 1963), Vol. III.